Western Civilization I

CLEP* Test Study Guide

All rights reserved. This Study Guide, Book and Flashcards are protected under the US Copyright Law. No part of this book or study guide or flashcards may be reproduced, distributed or stored in a retrieval system, or transmitted in any form or by any means, electronic, mechanical, photocopying, recording, or otherwise, without the prior written permission of the publisher Breely Crush Publishing, LLC.

© 2026 Breely Crush Publishing, LLC

*CLEP is a registered trademark of the College Entrance Examination Board which does not endorse this book.

971010420143

Copyright ©2003 - 2026, Breely Crush Publishing, LLC.

All rights reserved.

This Study Guide, Book and Flashcards are protected under the US Copyright Law. No part of this publication may be reproduced, distributed or stored in a retrieval system, or transmitted in any form or by any means, electronic, mechanical, photocopying, recording, or otherwise, without the prior written permission of the publisher Breely Crush Publishing, LLC.

Published by Breely Crush Publishing, LLC
10808 River Front Parkway
South Jordan, UT 84095
www.breelycrushpublishing.com

ISBN-10: 1-61433-654-7
ISBN-13: 978-1-61433-654-9

Printed and bound in the United States of America.

*CLEP is a registered trademark of the College Entrance Examination Board which does not endorse this book.

Table of Contents

Ancient Near East *1*
   Egypt and Mesopotamia at a Glance *1*
   Egyptian Political History *2*
   Law of Babylon *4*
   Hanging Gardens *4*
Ancient Greece & Hellenistic Civilization *5*
   Dark Ages of Greek *5*
   Evolution of Athens *7*
   Early Reforms *8*
   Greek Philosophy and Science *9*
   Greek Wars *10*
Ancient Rome *11*
   Early Republic *11*
   Punic Wars *11*
   Rome in Third Century *12*
   Trade in Third Century *12*
   German Invasion *12*
Medieval History *14*
   Byzantium and Islam *14*
   Islam *15*
   Early Medieval Politics and Culture Through Charlemagne *17*
   Economic and Social Condition of Western Europe in the Early
      Medieval Period *18*
   Feudal and Manorial Institutions *18*
   Rise of Towns and Changing Economic Forms *20*
   Medieval Thought and Culture *21*
   Feudal Monarchies *23*
   The Medieval Church *24*
Renaissance and Reformation *26*
   Renaissance in Italy *26*
   Protestantism and Catholicism Reformed and Reorganized *29*
Early Modern Europe, 1560-1648 .... *31*
   The Opening of the Atlantic *31*
   The Commercial Revolution *32*
   Dynastic and Religious Conflicts *33*
   Thought and Culture *34*
Western Civilization Since 1648 .... *36*
Absolutionism and Constitutionalism, 1648-1715 .... *36*

The "Westernization" of Russia *40*
Competition for Empire and Economic Expansion *41*
Global Economy of the 18th Century *41*
Sample Test Questions *42*
Test Taking Strategies *71*
What Your Score Means *72*
Test Preparation *72*
Legal Note *73*

Ancient Near East

EGYPT AND MESOPOTAMIA AT A GLANCE

PThe debate is still hot over which is the most ancient civilization. For most scholars, it's the Egyptian civilization but to some archaeologists, it is the Mesopotamian civilization. Both these civilizations have some remarkable similarities.

   a) Both had an organized society and some sort of administration
   b) Both developed their skills in the field of art and science
   c) Both relied on rivers for their crops

Primitive civilizations grew and flourished mostly in river valleys. Egyptian civilization flourished in the valley of the river Nile. The Nile was also considered as the lifeline of Egyptian civilization. Every year, the Nile would lay a fresh layer of alluvial deposits over its banks for the Egyptians to grow their crops. Nile valley was very productive and farmers used to grow up to three crops in a single year. Some statistics of Egyptian civilization are given below:

Stretch 750 miles

Maximum Width 32 miles

Minimum Width 10 miles

Total Area 10,000 square miles

Mesopotamia was also gifted with many natural conditions. Two rivers, Tigris and Euphrates, supplied water for irrigation and transportation. Mesopotamia is a Greek word meaning "between the rivers". Separation between the two rivers was less than nineteen miles at some points and not more than forty miles at other places. As Mesopotamia was surrounded by desert, their territory was not scattered. This contributed in one way, building closely-knit societies; in fact, theirs were the first organized towns.

Climatic conditions also played a major role in the exponential growth of these two civilizations as compared to other parts of the world. There was great variation in temperature in different seasons. Nile temperature fluctuated between 60 degrees Fahrenheit in winter to 115 degrees Fahrenheit in summer.

Annual rainfalls were sporadic but floods compensated to loss of moisture and replenishing of fertile land.

Another good factor supporting the Egyptian civilization was the absence of malaria in most of the Egyptian towns.

Wind mostly flowed in the opposite direction to the flow of Nile; this benefited upstream trade and proved to be great help in transportation.

On the other side, weather was little harsher in Mesopotamia. Scorching heat started to fall with the onset of summer. Humidity levels were also higher as compared to Egypt, and the desert was drier. Seasonal wind currents provided right timing for the ripening of fruits. Date and dietary staples were the chiefly harvested crops in Mesopotamia.

Melting peaks of the north produced annual floods in the plains of Babylon. They too replenished the fertility of soil like the Nile did for Egypt.

EGYPTIAN POLITICAL HISTORY

Historians divide history of Egypt in six eras:

a) The Archaic or the Early Dynastic Period
b) The Old Kingdom
c) The First Intermediate Period
d) The Middle Kingdom
e) The Second Intermediate Period
f) The New Kingdom

Although the archaic period was regarded as the first age of Egyptian civilization, considerable advancements in the fields of society and politics were made even before it.

There are evidences to support the fact that Egyptians were using rational ways of irrigation and drainage. Copper tools were also present even before the Archaic period.

In 3100 BC, the unification of Egypt took place. Northern and Southern Egyptian parts were united to form a single dynasty.

It is believed that writing was also invented at this time for keeping records of the newly formed state. Unification had far-reaching influence on Egyptian society by both political and social means. It provided for a stronger civilization and centralized irrigation plans.

Greek Mythology gives credit to Narmer for this unification whereas Egyptian records credit Menes. Some historians believed that unification stretched for many generations.

Zoser, the mighty king of United Egypt who ruled around 2770 BC, was regarded as the founder of Old Kingdom. The first pyramids were built by Zoser.

There was no separation of religion and politics. Pharaohs were considered as sons of God Sun and were chief priests. Priests were the chief advisors of Pharaohs.

Salient features of the Old Kingdom

a) State followed the principles of peace and non-aggression.
b) There was no army for the state.
c) There was no national militia for the pharaohs or the state.
d) Local bodies were governed by civil officials.
e) Localities had their own militias.

Foreign rulers, the Hyksos, invaded Egypt around 1750 BC. They were primarily from western Asia. Internal disturbances and the tyranny of nobles made their task of conquering Egypt easier, as did their sophisticated knowledge of warfare and methods of travel like horses and chariots.

West Asian invaders left their mark on Egyptian culture by providing them skills for improved warfare. This made the foundation of a successful kingdom that would evolve over the centuries to come.

Ahmose, the King of the Eighteenth Dynasty liberalized Egypt from the foreign rule. Power slipped from the hands of nobles to Ahmose, who founded a more patriotic nation.

Ramses III was the last great Pharaoh of Egypt. He ruled from 1182 to 1151 BC.

Libyan barbarians ruled Egypt for more than two centuries. They were succeeded by Ethiopians from the upper parts of river Nile.

Assyrians conquered Egypt in 670 BC.

From the middle of the tenth century to nearly the end of the eighth, a dynasty of Libyan barbarians occupied the throne of the Pharaohs. The Libyans were followed by a line of Ethiopians or Nubians, who came in from the desert regions west of the Upper Nile. In 670, Egypt was conquered by the Assyrians, who succeeded in maintaining their supremacy for eight years only. After the collapse of Assyrians, Egyptians regained their independence, and a brilliant renaissance of culture ensued.

Assyrian art had great detail and paid special attention to lions and horses.

LAW OF BABYLON

Hammurabi, the famous Babylonian king, was the pioneer in giving law to mankind. This Code of Hammurabi formed the basis of their distinct system of law. His code was followed in its exact form or in its variant form by Babylonians, Assyrians, Chaldeans and the Hebrews.

Some basic features of Hammurabi Laws were:

(1) Law of Retaliation: Accused would be punished equivalently to his crime, An Eye for an Eye, A Tooth for a Tooth and An Arm for an Arm.

(2) Role of Citizens: State cannot sentence anyone for any crime if he was not brought to justice by the victim's family. It was a kind of semi-private legal system.

(3) Inequality before the Law: This was another feature of Hammurabi's law. Residents were divided into three classes - Aristocrats, Common Population and Slaves. Sentences were based on the rank or position of the offender and that of a victim. Crime was considered serious if Aristocrats were involved in it; either as victim or as offender. Punishments were severe for upper class people, if they were found guilty.

(4) No distinction between Intentional and Accidental Crime.

HANGING GARDENS

The Hanging Gardens of Babylon are said to be one of the seven wonders of the ancient world. They were built by the Chaldean king Nebuchadnezzar II around 600 BC for his sick wife and were destroyed by earthquakes about 400 years later.

Ancient Greece & Hellenistic Civilization

Greeks were the first people who refused to submit to the rules of dictator priests. They were firm believers in the gods, but were not overly superstitious. They were highly secular and rational in thoughts.

DARK AGES OF GREECE

1100 BC to 800 BC was the most unfortunate period for Greeks. This period is also referred as the dark age of Greek civilization. After the fall of Mycenaean Civilization, Greek civilization crept into a period of chaos and uncertainty.

All the written records of early Greek were destroyed in the Dark Ages. Only those few records that were stored accidentally were available.

Cultural and social developments were rolled back to their primitive forms. Business and trade was virtually wiped out from Greece. The barter system regained strength. There were no merchants in Greece during the dark ages.

RELIGION DURING THE DARK AGES

For the citizens of Greece during the Dark Ages, religion was considered as a system for accounting for the physical activities around them in a simplified form:

a) Explaining human nature;

b) A means for obtaining physical comforts in the form of good fortune, better life, skilled manpower and so on;

c) Religion was not a savior from their worldly sins.

POLITICS DURING THE DARK AGES

During the Dark Ages, entity of state as a body was reduced to non-existence. Local bodies were autonomous in all states and by all means. Each little community was a state in itself. The tribal leader was also the ruler but without power except as an army chief during wars and as the chief priest at the time of worship. He too had to cultivate his farm like any other farmer and the community had no liability to offer him anything.

LAW DURING DARK AGES

There was no written law in the Dark Ages. It was left to the victim's family to punish the offender. Community had no role in implementing justice. Though the tribal leader resolved disputes, his role during the proceedings was that of a mediator only.

SOCIAL AND ECONOMIC LIFE IN DARK AGES

Social and economic life was simple throughout the Dark Ages. There was no classification as that of aristocrats, priests or any other form. Hard work and manual labor were a must for everyone and it was not looked upon as symbol of lower status. No one possessed enough assets to be called rich. Although, there were some landlords, primarily nobles and serfs worked on their land. There is no marked evidence to prove that slaves worked on the fields. Women were mostly hired as slaves for working as servants, and for collecting and processing wool.

Agriculture was the chief source of income for almost everyone.

HOMER AND THE ILIAD

Homer wrote the Iliad, an epic narrative. The story is set during a war between the Greeks and the Trojans. The war began because Helen was kidnapped from Sparta. Achilles is the main character of the story. Because Achilles is affronted by his superior officer, he withdraws from the war, leaving the rest of the army to fail in his absence. Though they try to reconcile, Achilles chooses not to return but allows his friend to lead his regimen in his place. The friend is killed and Achilles is very upset. He turns these emotions towards the Trojans. He then kills their leader in a one on one fight.

At the time, the military was very important. Between the ages of eight and thirteen, boys would go to pre-basic training. When they reached the age of thirteen, they lived in the barracks with the other soldiers until they were thirty years old. Those who were at least twenty years old could get married but still had to live in the barracks until thirty . Those who were between the ages of thirty and sixty-five were subject to recall, like the reserves. They call Helen of Troy the face that launched a thousand ships because a ten-year war was fought over her.

The citizens of the city of Troy were called Trojans. The Greeks made a large horse, secretly filled with their troops. They made the rest of their camps disappear, creating the illusion that they had conceded the war. The Trojans took the spectacular horse as a gift and brought it into the city. That night the entire city celebrated their victory. After the citizens fell asleep, the Greeks came out of the horse, killed the guards at the gate and let in their fellow soldiers who then leveled the city. This maneuver henceforth was known as the Trojan Horse.

HOMER'S ODYSSEY

The Odyssey is about the Greek hero Odysseus that is coming home from the Trojan War. While he's been at war, many things have happened in his home. There are suitors staying at his home that are trying to woo his wife, Penelope. Penelope weaves and unravels it at night to show that time is not passing. Odysseus has been gone for ten years. In those years he had to face many things including a man-eating on-eyed-giant named Polyphemus, son of Poseidon. Odysseus (also known as Ulysses) puts a beam in the fire, gets it sharp and puts it in the eye of the monster. He also dealt with Calypso, a siren who offers him immortality if he will stay with her and not return home. When Odysseus returns he tests the loyalty of his servants, plots and carries out a bloody revenge on Penelope's suitors, and is reunited with his family.

EVOLUTION OF ATHENS

There is no evidence of any armed invasion of Athens. Other factors that led to the development of Athens as one great nation are:

1. No biasing of communities; hence no bitter opposition or conflicts.
2. Athens was free from military dictatorship.

3. Athens was rich in mineral deposits.
4. Some excellent harbors also contributed to the development of Athens.
5. From the onset, Athens was a business center, not an agricultural state.

POLITICS IN EARLY ATHENS

Athens also had a monarchial form of rule till the middle of Eighth century BC. But soon, the Council of Nobles gained power and deprived the king of most of his powers.

Council of Nobles was called Areopagus.

Formation of Areopagus was a direct consequence of increasing wealth of Athens and empowerment of traders.

AGRICULTURE IN ATHENS

Another great achievement of Athens was its vineyards and olive yards. Both vine and olive yards were maintained by big landlords as it took considerable time before the first crop of vine and olive were harvested. Price of grain was falling sharply as Athens was importing it at lower rates.

Farmers often had to mortgage their land to escape from heavy debts. This led many farmers to become slaves when they were not able to pay the loan.

EARLY REFORMS

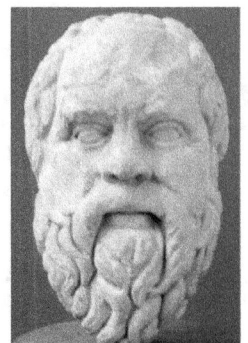

With the onset of Fifth Century BC, Athens saw reforms to redeem the farmers from their miseries. A council of all parties passed a bill to empower Solon as chief magistrate in order to carry out successful reforms. Some salient features of these reforms were:

a) Formation of a new council with 400 members and allowing middle class families to take membership

b) Allowing lower class representatives in the assembly

c) Formation of a court of appeal against criminal cases where all citizens had the right to appeal.

GREEK PHILOSOPHY AND SCIENCE

Greek Philosophy started to gain shape in the early sixth century BC. The origin of Greek Philosophy is associated with the Milesian School. Philosophy at that time was chiefly scientific. Almost all discussions were centered on composition of the earth and human beings.

Thales was the founder of the School. According to him, every single substance on this planet originated from moisture.

At the end of sixth century BC, Greek Philosophy shifted towards metaphysical approach. Now apart from composition of matter, the Nature of human beings was also discussed. Discussions were now centered on

- Truth
- Divinity
- Human Nature
- Harmony
- Good and Evil

The first atomic theory was given by Atomists. Atomists were renowned philosophers of second half of fifth century. They postulated that matter consisted of small particles. They elaborated that atoms were the fundamental building blocks that combine in very large numbers to form matter. Atoms cannot be destructed.

Democritus was the first to deny the existence of any spiritual world. He strongly resented the concept of the immortality of the soul.

Sophists had the most profound effect on Greek Philosophy in Fifth Century. Sophists strongly opposed slavery and racial discrimination. Protagoras was a leading Sophist.

Socrates was one of the most renowned philosophers of Greek. He was born in 469 BC. Socrates never had any formal education in philosophy. He was the son of a sculptor. He strongly opposed the thoughts and beliefs of Sophists and was sentenced to death in 399 BC.

Plato was a student of Socrates who conveyed his thoughts and beliefs to the rest of the world. Plato wrote books like The Apology, The Phaedo, The Phaedrus, The Symposium and The Republic.

Pericles (461-429 BC)
Pericles was the first king who formed true democracy in Athens. During his tenure, the assembly got powers to stand against the decisions of the council. The assembly also gained special rights to initiate any proposal or legislation. Another council, similar to a cabinet, was also formed. Members of this council were Great Generals. Generals were from the Army, highly placed Executives and other walks of life with special achievements. Total number of members in this council was ten. Members were chosen for a period of one year by the assembly members.

Pericles placed himself as the leader of Board of Generals. He ruled this board for more than 30 years.

Another achievement of Pericles was the formation of an organized system of law. Pericles formed a hierarchical chain of courts starting at the lowest level of popular courts.

GREEK WARS

Two major wars in the fourth century, the Persian War (490-479 BC) and the Peloponnesian War (431-404 BC) decided the fate of Greek civilization. These wars were technically fought by only Athens and their allies, but due to the far-reaching consequences on the entire Greek civilization, these were called the Great Wars of Greece.

The cause of the Persian War was nothing but an early facet of the growing imperialism. Athens was the major player in this war. Athens supported the Ionian, speaking cities in the Asia Minor, in their freedom quest against Persia. Persia attacked Athens as a counter strategy. Persian attack loomed as a shadow of fear for the entire Greek culture. It was Athens which bore maximum threat and responsibility of the war.

Athens retaliated in a furious manner and claimed great victories like that in Marathon and Salamis. Persia was defeated and a stronger Democratic Athens emerged.

The Second Great War was fought between Athens and Sparta. Historians see the imperialistic desires of Athens as the main cause behind this war.

Athens formed a league of different states called the Delian League to fight the tyranny of Persia. Delian League was the joint army of different Greek states, including Sparta and Mau.

Ancient Rome

EARLY REPUBLIC

Before the formation of the Republic, Roman Society was divided into two classes social classes, the Patricians and the Plebeians.

Patricians were the upper class landlords, aristocrats, and wealthy businessmen. Plebeians were small landlords, farmers and small businessmen. Plebeians were of foreign origin and settled in different cities of Rome. Senate and magistrate offices were under the direct hold of Patricians. Plebeians were exploited by the patricians to work on their lands, pay heavy taxes and to fight for them in wars. Plebeians had no rights in the senate but were members of the assembly.

Plebeians' uprising gained momentum in 494 BC and they forced Patricians to elect Tribunes, local plebeian officers who could veto the decision of Magistrate.

In 450 BC, 12 tables of law were published because of Plebeian protest, which gave citizens of Rome the right to appeal.

In 367 BC, the first Plebeian council was elected. Plebeians were also eligible to contest for Magistrate.

PUNIC WARS

Rome fought three wars with Carthage which became famously known as the Punic Wars of Rome. Carthage was a Great Empire on the northern coast of Africa. Their enormous wealth and strong navy where envied by the Romans. Moreover, Carthage was an ambitious empire and their expansion created trouble for Rome.

The First War with Carthage, also known as the First Punic War, broke out in 264 BC. It lasted for twenty-three years and Rome emerged as the victorious state.

The Second Punic War was fought in 218 BC when Carthaginians tried to build a Spanish Empire. This war lasted for sixteen years and ended with Carthage surrendering most of its territory, assets and paying three times more indemnification as paid in First War of Carthage. Hannibal, the great Carthaginian General, led this war on behalf of Carthage.

The Third Punic War was fought between 149-146 BC. It was the bloodiest Punic War and ended with the devastation of Carthage and all its citizens being enslaved.

JULIUS CAESAR (100-44 BC)

Caesar's fame started to grow with his victories over Gaul. At one time, Caesar was announced as the enemy of state by the conspiracies of Pompey, his political rival whom he defeated in 48 BC in Pharsalus.

Caesar conquered Asia Minor soon after defeating Pompey. In 46 BC, he declared himself as the next ruler of Rome. He was assassinated by a group of conspirators in 44 BC.

ROME IN THIRD CENTURY

Imperial rule of the great Roman Empire came to an end in the third century. Marcus Aurelius was the last successful king among the Five Good Emperors. He was succeeded by Commodus.

TRADE IN THIRD CENTURY

Roman trade expanded to nearly all parts of the world including India, Arabia and China. Items like clothes, artifacts and glass were exported at that time. Heavy export of these goods did not make any contribution to the prosperity of Rome. Roman Economy was crippled and wealth distributed unevenly.

Availability of slaves declined and hence production too. On the other hand, imports for the luxury of rich and elite were too heavy to be countered by domestic export. Consequently, the Roman Economy began to be crushed under its own imports.

GERMAN INVASION

In the third century, Roman Civilization faced two assaults, one from Christianity and another from Germans. German invaders were always a threat for Roman Civilization. Diocletian and Theodosius the great were successful in keeping Germans away from Rome, but their successors failed to do so. By the fifth century, Germans invaded all of western Rome.

German invaders, also called barbarians by some historians, were similar to Romans in many ways. Although they were illiterate and did not live in cities like Romans, their appearance and customs were similar to that of neighboring Romans. Living for centuries in close vicinity to Rome, left some impression on them. Primarily they were hunters and grazers but they did practice some sort of cultivation to meet their food needs. Unlike Romans who used copper, Germans used iron for making jewelry and pottery.

Geographical conditions were also responsible for the German invasion. Rome and Germany were situated next to each other with only Rhine and Danube separating them. Rome had a long trading history with some of the German tribes. More than often, left-over Roman fields were acquired by the bordering tribes of Germany.

Strategically, Germans played an important role in Roman warfare by allying with Roman armies to fight other Germanic tribes.

The most important thing that brought the Germans closer to Rome was the adoption of Christianity. By the onset of the Fourth Century, most of the German tribes adopted the heretical Arian Christianity. They no longer considered themselves as barbarians. Hence their ambition for getting into the heart of Rome gained even more momentum.

Ruling Rome was not the primary motive of Germans. They were looking for more lands that could give them better yields every year. In the last quarter of the Fourth Century, tribe of Visigoths revolted against Roman officials and finally defeated their army in the war of Adrianople.

After the victory of Adrianople in 378, Germans formed friendly relations with the ruling emperor of Rome, Theodosius the Great, and remained on friendly terms till his death. After the death of Theodosius in 395, his kingdom was divided between his two incompetent sons. Alaric, the leader of Visigoths at that time, acted wisely and selected the best lands and provisions for his tribe. Very soon, a great portion of Rome was acquired by Germans much to the envy of their neighbors.

In 406, Vandals and Visigoths lead a combined attack on Gaul to enter straight into Spain. After sometime, they crossed the straits into the northwestern territories of Roman Africa. At that time, it was the most heavily harvested land of the Roman Empire and the victory brought Rome to its knees. The German march of victory did not end here. They also won Central Mediterranean by defeating the Roman Navy in 455.

Last blow to the great civilization of Rome came in the year 476, when a group of Germans sacked the non-existent king of Rome, Augustulus, a boy in his teens, to gain control of the entire Rome, forever.

Medieval History

BYZANTIUM AND ISLAM

BYZANTIUM

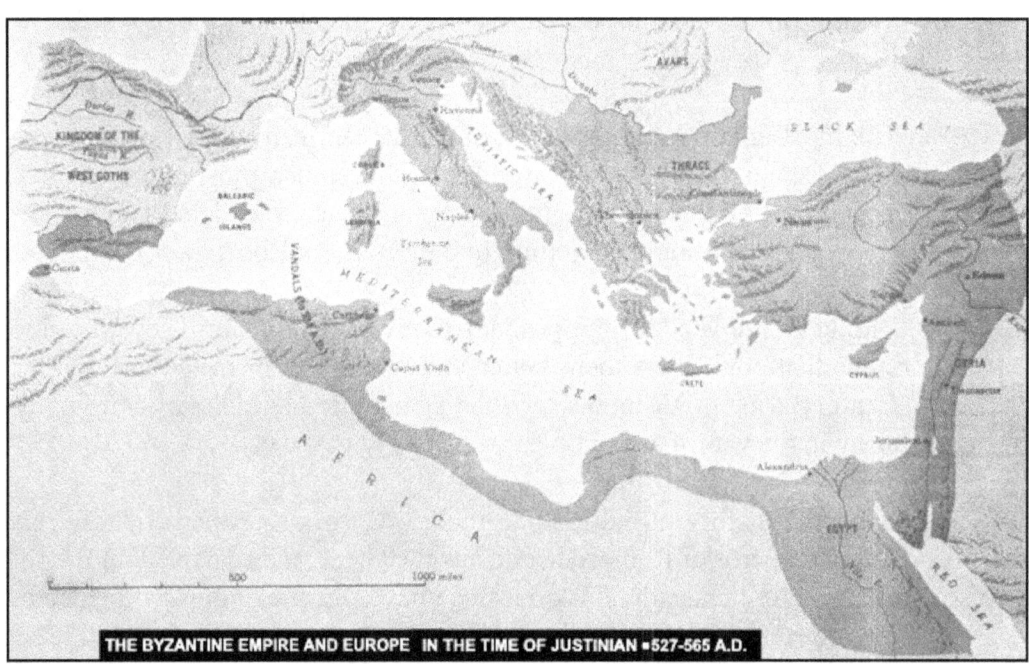

THE BYZANTINE EMPIRE AND EUROPE IN THE TIME OF JUSTINIAN ▪ 527-565 A.D.

In 700, three civilizations emerged from different parts of Mediterranean Sea: Byzantine, Islam and western Christianity. All these were considered as successors of Roman civilization. The story of Byzantine civilization has many twists and turns. The origin of the Byzantine Empire is not clear yet, but it is believed that this civilization succeeded the Roman civilization.

The arrival of the Justinian reign had great impact upon the Byzantine civilization as it marked the beginning of new thoughts and practices.

FACTORS RESPONSIBLE FOR THE STABILITY OF THE BYZANTINE EMPIRE

The most important cause for the stability of the Byzantine Empire was the intricate and tricky backstage machinations. Another reason was the highly efficient and active bureaucrats. The third factor was the stable economic firms. Despite the decline of urban life in most of the western countries, the eastern part of Byzantine had a solid commerce and city life. The Byzantine Empire had also a good source of income through their silk-making business.

Agriculture during the Byzantine civilization was of great importance as it was the greatest source of income. The concept of free peasantry vanished with the arrival of aristocrats in 1025.

Byzantine civilization is also remembered for its religious beliefs and practices. The Byzantine civilization had a complicated religious dimension, as the emperors of those days had interfered in the workings of the church. It was during the eighth century that religious practices saw some stability because of the decline of many eastern provinces.

Another issue related to the religion of Byzantine civilization was the iconoclastic movement. The iconoclasts strongly believed that images made by man himself cannot be worshipped, and Christ is so great that no one can portray his exact image, thus worshipping icons should be prohibited.

Byzantine civilization had some very special things. One is that Byzantine civilization showed equal concern to Greek teachings and Christianity. It also contributed to women's education.

ARCHITECTURE DURING BYZANTINE CIVILIZATION
The architecture of this period can best be realized through the Church of Santa Sophia. It symbolizes the inward and spiritual character of the Christian religion. The structure of this monument was different from others constructed at that time. Most of the art and architecture of the Byzantine civilization were based on the ancient Greek style. The Byzantines are popularly remembered for their ivory paintings, jewelry making and creation of mosaics. A mosaic is a picture which is made by assembling many small pieces of glass or stone.

With the passage of time, Byzantine's ties with Russia improved. But, its relations with the West were bitter. In 1204, when Constantinople was sacked, its relation with the West became the worst. Taking the advantage of the situation, Turks conquered Constantinople in 1453.

The hatred of Byzantine for Islam helped the west to preserve Greek learning.

ISLAM

THE GROWTH OF ISLAM, ISLAMIC CIVILIZATION AND CULTURE

Islamic civilization began in the seventh century in Arabia.

Muhammad, the founder of Islam, was born in Mecca. He emphasized that the divine god is supreme and all men and women should surrender themselves to this divine power.

After the death of Muhammad, Arabians found difficulty in selecting the head of the Muslim community, and later declared Abu-Bakr as their religious leader, Caliph. In 636, Umar, another Caliph, defeated Byzantine and captured cities like Jerusalem and Damascus, and later in the year 637, they destroyed the Persian army and moved to the capital of Ctesiphon. During the entire medieval period, the Islamic power continued to shift between different Caliphs, like Umar, Umayyad, Abbasid, etc. During the period between 935 and the 16th century, Islamic politics saw many different small rulers.

Before the introduction of Islam, Arabia was considered as a small desert land, and people earned their livelihood by selling camel's milk or cultivating date palms, etc. In the middle of the 6th century, the economic life started improving due to the growth and development of trade. Traders and businessmen moved with manufactured goods like cotton clothes, jewelry, pottery, and silks to China, India, and Southern Russia.

ISLAMIC RELIGION

The religion of Islam resembles both Judaism and Christianity, but the absence of clergy brings it closer to the former. Islamic culture is considered to be dynamic and wide, spread across the world. It had whole-heartedly embraced the sophistication of both Byzantium and Persia. Islam made great effort in relating religious beliefs and basic requirements of life.

The religion had different thoughts regarding the rights for women. Muslim men consider their women as their own property and expect them to follow all their commands, without any complaint or argument. The followers of Islam were divided into two religious groups, Ulama and Sufis. While Ulama believed in maintaining tradition and faith, Sufis believed in meditation and happiness.

ISLAMIC PHILOSOPHY

Islamic philosophy was based upon the thoughts of Aristotle and the great Napoleon. The period between 850 and 1200 is considered as the golden period of Islamic philosophy. Islamic philosophers or, the faylasufs, were finding difficulty in correlating the Greek and Islamic philosophy. Islamic philosophers were eminent astrologers and proficient in the field of medicine.

ISLAMIC ART AND ARCHITECTURE

The Islamic art and architecture were unique and popular. Most of their art works were based on the art of Byzantium and Persia. Most of the construction of domes, horseshoe arches, and twisted columns, resembles Byzantium art, while decorative motifs were very close to Persian art. The pictures and sculptures were rich in geometric designs, fruits, flowers, etc.

ISLAMIC TECHNOLOGY

Westerners were highly influenced by the Islamic technology and adopted techniques for irrigation, paper making, and distillation of alcohol. Islamic civilization indeed is recognized for its brilliant heritage of original discoveries and achievements.

EARLY MEDIEVAL POLITICS AND CULTURE THROUGH CHARLEMAGNE

Western Europe in the starting of the medieval age (600 to 1050) was diffident, still a number of dynasties and monarchies were coming into existence. During 687, many powers like Pepin of Heristal were able to join together all the Frankish lands and reconstruct a new power in Belgium and the Rhine. However, the best alliance came during the period of Charlemagne, son of Pepin, who marked the beginning of new era in the medieval period.

THE REIGN OF CHARLEMAGNE (768 TO 814)

Charlemagne soon realized that in order to extend the Frankish monarchy, he needed educated people and thus stressed what was to become the Carolingian Renaissance. Realizing that people in Europe were illiterate and ignorant, he took the help of Anglo-Saxon Benedictine Alucin, when he was planning to extend his empire in Germany. During 800, when Charlemagne was crowned emperor, he did not gain any power as the Franks were gaining power at the same time.

The period, however, saw some great changes as he was able to bring victory and internal peace. Despite giving so many contributions in Europe, the successors of Charlemagne were unable to create the same magic. The situation became worse when conflict between the family members started and the Carolingian empire lost its identity and Europe saw a completely new modern political scenario in the 10th century.

AFTER THE DECLINE OF CHARLEMAGNE

The biggest change that occurred after the decline of the Carolingian empire was England united as one country under the rule of King Alfred. Similarly, France was divided into small fragments as it was unable to resist the continuous attack of successors of Charlemagne. Germany emerged as the most powerful continent and Otto relieved Germany from foreign threats.

THE EMPIRE OF CHARLEMAGNE 814 A.D.

ECONOMIC AND SOCIAL CONDITIONS IN WESTERN EUROPE IN THE EARLY MEDIEVAL PERIOD

The European economy was agriculture-based between the 8th and 11th century. During this period, the main economic unit was the large estates owned by the emperors, warriors, and so on. Although the North European soil was fertile, due to lack of modern tools, peasants were unable to produce good yield of crops. Thus, the economic condition of the masses was not good, which led to a poor social condition.

LITERATURE AND ART

The development in the field of literature was inadequate. Very few Christians were fond of writing. Those who were, were mainly monks who could not devote themselves to it full time because of their profession. However, there were many impressive piece of writings in Latin, most popular among them was the Anglo-Saxon epic poem *Beowulf*.

The Early Medieval age would not see much development in the field of art either. Between the 6th and 8th century some of the monuments made by monks in Ireland were significant. Paintings made by Irish monks mostly were anti-classical and surrealistic. Best among them was the "Book of Kells", which is remembered as the most stylish book of art. Since the tenth century, European civilization started changing and it became clear that, very soon, the West would emerge as the biggest power in the world.

FEUDAL AND MANORIAL INSTITUTIONS

Historians called the period between 1050 and 1300 the High Medieval Period. During this period, Western Europe came out of its backward and poor conditions and emerged as the supreme power of the world.

THE AGRICULTURE REVOLUTION

The period after 1050 is remembered for its agriculture revolution. When Europeans realized that the dry Mediterranean soil was unable to produce crops, they shifted to the north Atlantic region. With suitable climatic conditions and the latest cultivation tools, the economic conditions showed improvement.

MODERN AGRICULTURE TOOLS

Among the various modern tools used for cultivation, the important ones are the heavy plow, mills, horse shoes, horse collars, and so on. With the introduction of shoes and collars for horse, oxen were replaced by horses in the agriculture field. Other useful tools of that period were the wheel barrow, harrow etc. Farmers also adopted the three-crop rotation system.

MANORIAL REGIME

Growth in agricultural products led to an improved social and economic condition of both landlords and the peasants. The rural life in the high medieval period was completely based upon landlords and their manors. Manorialism is defined as an economic system, whereby the manor is owned by the landlord and serfs work upon the manor. Part of a manor is given to the serfs, so that they can grow crops for themselves and their families.

In the early period of high medieval period, serfs, though better than the Roman slaves, were not very happy working on the manors, as they were left with very little crops for themselves. But the situation became favorable for serfs when the landlords started opening new lands for laborers. The concept of laborers also attracted the serfs. Thus serfs managed to produce enough to live comfortably. However, serfdom came to an end during the 13th century.

The high medieval period also showed great improvement in lifestyle. As there were few wars and more economic growth, people started living a noble life. Chivalry too led to a much better life. Women received respect and were not treated as merely material for men, unlike in the Islamic reign.

GROWTH IN TRADE AND URBAN REVOLUTION

The agriculture revolution, improved economic and social condition also led to the development of trade. River, sea and land were used as the means of transportation. To further improve trade, construction of bridges and use of pack horses were introduced. With the development of trade, a new mode of payment - payment through money and coins - was started, and to sell goods, traders started displaying products at international trade fairs.

RISE OF TOWNS AND CHANGING ECONOMIC FORMS

During the twelfth century, Europe saw speedy development of towns throughout the country. Unlike the Roman period, the towns during the medieval period were rather large. Most of the urban life was confined to Italy, with some of the largest European cities being Venice, Milan, and Genoa. All these cities were densely populated.

CAUSE FOR THE MEDIEVAL URBAN REVOLUTION

The reinforcement of long distance trade was considered as the main cause for the urban revolution, though this was not true with all towns. Some towns like Venice

were hugely dependent on long distance trade, while many other towns depended completely on the wealth of nearby areas. All these helped them in bringing raw materials and large number of people to the town.

Both town and rural life survived hand in hand, as towns provided a market to goods manufactured by different artisans and rural life provided them food and more hands to work in factories.

With the passage of time, different towns became specialized in particular businesses. Paris became famous for universities and educational institutions, Venice concentrated in outside trade, Milan and other towns became manufacturers, especially producing clothes.

However, one cannot say that the medieval towns were like the towns of the modern times, due to lack of knowledge and progression in certain areas. People did not know much about proper housekeeping, cleanliness and drainage systems. Lack of cleanliness and awareness led to many diseases and mortality among town dwellers.

SOCIAL AND ECONOMIC ORGANIZATION OF THE TOWN

The medieval town had guilds, the most common among them were merchant and craft guild. Through guilds, organizations and associations were established to promote and protect the interests of town dwellers. The role of the merchant guild was to control the market and preserve a stable economic system. The role of craft guild was to look after the issues and matters related to craftsmen and artisans.

Overall, both types of guilds helped in maintaining uniformity in the price of the goods, deciding working hours, suggesting and implementing different methods of production and quality of products.

The development of town in the high medieval period will be always remembered for the resultant growth in life, economy and standard of living of the dwellers. This also introduced the new government system. Towns also helped in the development of schools and universities and increased the literacy rate in Western Europe.

MEDIEVAL THOUGHT AND CULTURE

Religious thought, culture and literature were also of great importance during the Medieval periods. Papal monarchy was considered as the most significant organization of that time, and Popes emerged as the supreme power. In the west they took the church under their control, confronted the kings and initiated crusading movements.

When the Carolingian empire declined, the decentralization of religious belief and corruption prevailed in all parts of Europe. During the tenth century, when external invasions became frequent in Europe, situations started changing. The first step in this regard was the acceptance of monasteries. The movement for monastic reforms resulted in the emergence of the monastery of Cluny in Burgundy.

In the mid-eleventh century, when secular authorities lost control of the monasteries, reformers started concentrating upon the clerical hierarchy, and refused simony - the purchase and sale of church. The most remarkable reform movements were during the preaching of Gregory VII. Acting like a revolutionary, he stood strongly against *lay investiture*.

Lay investiture is the practice in which secular rulers grant office to their clerks. This practice came to an end in 1122. Successors of Gregory VII were great followers of Papal monarchy and were interested in the day to day functioning of the church. With the passage of time, Popes managed to gain power and control of the church. It was their prerogative to appoint Bishops and general councils to disseminate laws and watch their headship.

Papal monarchy is best remembered for achievements like having control over the working of church, help in bringing uniformity in the religious practices, and also for international communication. Papal monarchy is also responsible for the rise and fall of different crusading movements. The first crusade started by the Pope also became the reason for their victory.

With the large numbers of people entering the new monasteries came the arrival of new religion and devotion. One was the more wide spread devotion to the Virgin Mary. While these devotions had existed since the early days of the church, they held a great significance in medieval times as a women held a renewed place of honor in Christianity. Also, artists and writers placed a greater importance on the Virgin Mary and started writing about her family life, women's feelings and emotions. All these new practices gave birth to new devotion.

During the end of the thirteenth century, Papal monarchy had a close relationship with the Franciscan and Dominican orders Popes supported the friars in gaining power in Europe and permitted them to violate the duties of the parish priests.

EDUCATION DURING THE HIGHER MEDIEVAL PERIOD

Four major accomplishments in the field of education during this period were the stress on spreading primary education and literacy, emergence and spread of universities, acceptance and promotion of Islamic knowledge and bringing various thoughts of Westerners into reality. This age also saw the introduction of cathedral schools and the content of curriculum was increased.

It was during the end of twelfth and the beginning of thirteenth century that lay education became popular as the church had no control over education. Thus education became secular and attracted different types of people. Another reason for its popularity was the growth of lay schools along side church schools.

Another remarkable achievement in this field was the tremendous growth in scientific and speculative thought, and also the emergence of Scholasticism. Scholasticism was defined as the method of teaching in the medieval period; however, it was also explained as the way to understand the whole world.

LITERATURE DURING THE HIGH MEDIEVAL PERIOD

The literature of the High Medieval Period in the west was considered the best and more broadly based than any literature during any other period. With the cathedral school education and knowledge of grammar, poets were able to create some remarkable pieces of Latin poetry of that time.

The best among them were the poetry written by Goliards, a group of poets. Their poetry touched on everything from nature to the joy of life. Poets not only used Latin, but also French, Spanish, German, and other languages. During the twelfth century, poems were written about different things in different styles. Among the various popular poems of that time, *The Divine Comedy* by A. Dante is remembered as one of the best.

ARCHITECTURE DURING THE HIGH MEDIEVAL PERIOD

The High Medieval Period also saw great achievements and developments in the field of architecture. During the tenth century, Romanesque, a form of architecture, was introduced, which gained popularity during the eleventh and twelfth century. Initially, it was introduced as an art to show the glory of God in religious constructions by depicting each of the architectural details uniformly. Other features of this art were huge walls of stone, plenty of piers, small windows and overuse of horizontal lines. This art was spread in the latter half of eleventh and twelfth century by the Gothic. Later, Gothic emerged with its own style of architecture, which also became very popular.

The High Medieval Period also saw growth and development in the field of drama and music. Most of the western music was homophonic, but in the high medieval period, polyphonic music was introduced, which later became the concept of counterpoint.

FEUDAL MONARCHIES

Both France and England emerged as stable dynasties, with feudal emperors as the rulers during the period of the 12th and 13th centuries. During those days, feudal lords became the supreme power and had complete control over landlords and thus, other men holding any powerful post became their subordinates.

ENGLAND

After the death of the Anglo-Saxon ruler Edward, William, the Duke of Normandy, was suggested to take the crown. However, this idea was not acceptable for some sections of the Anglo-Saxon assembly, as they wanted Harold Godwinsson to ascend the throne. This led the Norman invasion of England, a war in which William and his troop won the battle. William was very clever and artful. He was able to establish a strong kingdom and also lessen the powers and rights of the regional lords. It was during his regime that the traditional monarchy in England was converted into a legal monarchy. In order to collect taxes, he introduced the doomsday book, so that no one should ignore the tax collectors. After the death of William's son, and long fighting between the rebellions, a new empire was established by Henry II.

Magna Carta

The reign of Henry II was the worst in the history, as he believed in dictatorship, and thus killed many innocents. The successors of Henry II were also like him; they too imposed high taxes upon the people. In 1209, when John I was criticized for intervening in the working of Pops, he punished all his critics. This behavior and his defeat in war with France, made people rebellious and forced John I to acknowledge the Magna Carta. This limited the king's power and the right to collect tax came under the landlords.

It was after the twelfth century that England became one of the most well-governed feudal monarchies of the medieval period.

FRANCE

The feudal monarchy in France saw a very slow start. The French empire was developed in the year 987. It took quite a long time for France to solve its internal matters and concentrate on expanding its empire. During the regime of Phillip II Augustus, France was a secure place for the powers of kings. The king was treated as the head and all others were his subordinates. Very soon France sensed the motives of William II of England, and thus, attacked his troops. The battle continued for more than a hundred years.

Louis 9th, though with strong French troops, was unable to defeat England, but was recognized as a good emperor, as he managed to construct strong rules for tax, also eliminated serfdom and introduced the right of petition. The French dynasty also emphasized politeness, majesty, and other manners of the court.

GERMANY

Germany, like Italy, had not experienced strong feudal monarchies. Germany, with Burgundy, and Italy were assimilated in the Holy Roman Empire and were ruled by Hohenstaufens. The war continued for two years especially with the Papal monarchy, and proved that Germany had a weak monarchy.

RUSSIA

Russia appeared as a strong power in the west during the High Medieval Period. Most of the Russians had adopted Greek orthodox practices, and thus they became closer to Byzantines. During the eleventh century, Russian powers were affected due to aristocracy. During the thirteenth century, Russia came under the world of Islam by the Mongols. During the reign of Mongols, Russia was almost detached with the west. In 1480, Ivan the Great won over the Mongols, and conquered different parts of Russia.

THE MEDIEVAL CHURCH

The Church during the years 590 through 1517 had a strong group of Christians believing in the existence of God's hand in most of the happenings around them. Popes played an important role in building the church of the medieval period in Rome. With the passage of time the Church of Rome affected the entire European continent. The philosophy of this time was based upon struggle and academics.

The Christian Church was of supreme importance in the Middle Ages, and there was consequently a large amount of surviving material that relates to religious matters. The medieval churches were the common secular place where people could gather and talk, play and share their thoughts. People of this time had a strong belief in heaven and hell. They believed that if a man committed a sin and repented in front of Christ with sincere prayer, he would recieve mercy. This was equally believed by landlords as well as the peasants.

The owners of the church were very strong. The position of members of the church was arranged in order of hierarchy, and was highly influenced by the politics and the government. The clergies in the fourteenth century were the representatives of the Pope. The Papacy was superior to the rule of kings, and the Pope was often very influential and rich. The Papacy was the true protectors of the freedom of the church and thus were able to control the dictatorship of the king.

The rivalry between Thomas Becket, Archbishop of Canterbury and Henry II, is the best example of the enmity between the emperor and the church.

There were different forms of punishment for sin. People found committing sin or any unsocial, unethical activities, were ridiculed in front of the citizens; in some specific instances, the punishment was that heavy weights were placed at the back of the culprit. Another punishment was piercing an iron nail through the sinner's body, so that blood flowed from his body, but he would not die. Other methods were the punishment bench, paws of cats and racks.

Christians of that time had strong faith in pilgrimages, as they considered them to be the ultimate path to salvation. It was also the best way to unite people, and thus cultivate brotherhood and unity among them. Jerusalem was considered the best place, and Rome the next. England too had its share of fame, with the Canterbury shrine of St Thomas Becket, situated there. The pilgrims, while returning, carried holy water, coins or badges as memoirs. The relics too had great significance as they were believed to help in curing diseases.

POLITICAL POWER OF THE CHURCH

The Church was in a very good position, and was respected by all - kings, serfs, lords, freemen. Most of the churchmen had lands, some of them went to fight and served in the military.

During the Medieval period, the common practices was for all people from the king to freemen or serfs to pay 1/10th of their earnings to the Church. As a result, the church's economic condition improved, which resulted in corruption and other unsocial behavior. In the absence of any successors to the bishops, the lands and wealth accumulated by him were given to his friend and he was declared the new bishop by the king or else this was sold to someone else.

The church offices were also sold later on. That too created corruption and conflict between king, lords and the bishops. The power was divided between the kings and popes. In some area, the king was heard by everyone while in other places, Popes were more powerful.

If any Pope or churchmen were found guilty for committing sin or mistakes, they were thrown out of the church and severely punished.

Renaissance and Reformation

RENAISSANCE IN ITALY

In the later phase of the High Medieval Period, Italy emerged as the most advanced urban society among other countries of Europe. Renaissance in Italy was the result of advanced urban society, as most of the Italian aristocrats were living in urban cities and not on rural land.

The growth of the Renaissance in Italy was also due to the fact that it was very close to the established past than any other European city. The reason for being close to the past was that the cities, places and monuments present in the ancient Latin literature were quite close in resemblance to the cities in Italy. Also Italian scholars were trying hard to establish their own identity against scholasticism in France.

Strengthening the urban pride and per capita income were other reasons for the beginning of Renaissance in Italy.

RENAISSANCE OF THOUGHT AND LITERATURE

Francis Petrarch was the first Renaissance scholar in Italy. Petrarch explained that the ideal human behavior was to lead a simple life and perform meditation.

After Petrarch, many scholars stressed civic humanism. They believed that human life is incomplete without possessing earth and its different resources. These scholars also stressed the acceptance of Greek studies.

Another famous Italian scholar, Lorenzo Valla, spread the knowledge of grammar, rhetoric and in-depth analysis of Greek and Latin texts.

Between the years of 1450 and 1600, the school of Napoleanists in Italy spread the thought of Plato and other essential things regarding Christianity. The greatest political philosopher of the time was Niccolo Machiavelli. Castiglione was another popular philosopher, who defined the perfect Renaissance man as brave, witty, courteous and well educated.

RENAISSANCE ART

The Italian Renaissance had made great achievements in the field of art. The main reason was the discovery of the laws of linear perspective and its application in three dimensions. The artists of this century also mastered in learning the human anatomy, experienced the importance of different shades and light in art. They also introduced oil paints.

The painters of 15th century, in general, were Florentines, and the first among them was Masaccio. His art of imitating nature became the basis of renaissance paintings. Later, Florentine Sandro Botticelli was recognized as the true follower of Masaccio, and portrayed both religious and classical themes. The *Allegory of Spring* and *The Birth of Venus* were his famous pieces of art.

Another famous Florentine was Leonardo da Vinci, also recognized as the true Renaissance man. His paintings were known as the High Renaissance in Italy, and were true depiction of the nature. The period of High Renaissance also saw the emergence of the Venetian school. The most efficient painters of this school were Giovanni Bellini, Giorgione and Titian. Their paintings mostly were based upon the joy and life of Venice city.

The next half of the sixteenth century observed the emergence of other famous painters of High Renaissance. In fact, this period was considered the best for the art of renaissance Italy. Rome became the center of Italian art. Michelangelo of Florence was another famous painter, best known for his work on the Sistine Chapel and his statues of David and the Pieta, and with his death, the period of High Renaissance ended.

RENAISSANCE ARCHITECTURE

Renaissance architectural styles were very close to the past. The buildings constructed during this period were eclectic in shape, and most closely resembled that of the architecture of Medieval and Ancient Age. Renaissance architecture had an essence of

Neoplatonism, as they too believed in the fact that perfect proportion of man reflects the universe, and so did the buildings.

THE DECLINE OF RENAISSANCE IN ITALY

The period around 1550 saw the decline of Renaissance of Italy. The main causes for its declination were the French invasion in 1494, poor performance of Italian politics and counter-reformation.

THE RENAISSANCE OUTSIDE ITALY

During and after 1500, Renaissance started spreading in different parts of Europe, outside Italy. The situation in northern Europe after 1500 was favorable for the development of art and literature, thus north Europeans started learning from the development of Italy. Many Italian scholars moved to these areas and contributed to art and literature. The Renaissance inside and outside Italy, however, was not similar.

RENAISSANCE LITERATURE IN NORTHERN EUROPE

Artists, during the Renaissance, realized the art of Italy and started learning how to use the classical techniques in their art and left behind the Gothic styles of art. Among various artists of that time, Erasmus was remembered as the first and the most popular who contributed in the field of literature. He was totally against the Parisian style of scholasticism.

Erasmus' literature was both literary and doctrinal. Most of his writings were full of verbal effects. His works were a combination of both Latin and Greek. He was also good in adding fun to his writings, which made him popular among different groups of people. He explained all of his work as the philosophy of Christ.

Another famous artist of that time was Sir Thomas More, who is remembered for his literary piece called *Utopia*.

DECLINE OF CHRISTIAN HUMANISM

Despite all its great achievements and international recognition and acceptance, Protestant Reformation was lost in darkness. The Church's excessive corruption and religious practices forced the Protestants to take steps against them.

RENAISSANCE POETRY IN NORTHERN EUROPE

Northern Europe had experienced great achievements and development in the field of poetry during the sixteenth century. Poets like Pierre de Ronsard and Joachim de Bellay created beautiful epics in Petrarch's style.

Similarly, the famous poet Sir Philip Sidney, in England, created remarkable achievements in his poems by adopting and learning from Italian poems.

RENAISSANCE ARCHITECTURE IN NORTHERN EUROPE

The architecture of this time was remarkable, and is remembered for its uniqueness. French architects did great work by combining both the Gothic style as well as the classic horizontals in their construction. The result was magnificent Loire chateaux such as Amboise and Chambord.

French architects like Pierre Lescot took inspiration from the Italian work of architecture and constructed façades that stressed the classical pillars and pediment.

RENAISSANCE PAINTINGS IN NORTHERN EUROPE

Renaissance paintings too were of great importance, as they showed the perfect combination of art and thought. A famous painter of those days, Durer, learned the Italian style of proportion, perspective and modeling and put all of them in his paintings as well. He also learned the Italian style in portraying human beings as nude, but there was a great difference in his way of depicting nudity and that of the Italian style.

PROTESTANTISM AND CATHOLICISM REFORMED AND REORGANIZED

PROTESTANT REFORMATION (EARLY 1500 AND ALL OF THE 16TH CENTURY)

The growth of the Renaissance across Western Europe resulted in the growth of secular, or, worldly matters, in the Church, and believers like Martin Luther of traditional faith and religion strongly protested that. He believed that church should move with the traditional and old beliefs, as the new greed for power and worldly things were making them corrupt and insane. Soon, the protest triggered by Luther spread across the northern parts of Germany.

The result was a civil war in medieval Europe.

Not only Luther, but many others, especially those of the illicit urban middle class of Europe, like Calvin, protested against the church and its changing mindset. Calvin, popularly known for his Geneva reforms, had a difference in opinion with Luther in some of these matters.

Luther was in favor of followers of Christianity bearing the assessment of this life in anguish. However, Calvin believed that everyone should struggle throughout their life in the name of god. Calvin's thoughts were close and related to the old beliefs and faiths more than those of Luther's. While Luther accepted religious practices of Romans like altar and vestments, Calvin was against anything which was close to property.

THE RESULT OF PROTESTANT REFORMATION

The Protestant Reformers emphasized the use of the newly published edition of Bible. Protestant Reformation was completely rejected by the Christian humanists. According to them, nature of man is good, while Protestants felt it was polluted. Humanists emphasized refinement and acceptance, while Protestants had conviction and consistency in mind.

Protestant Reformation resulted in the super power of the sovereign state. Germany, England, Denmark, all adopted Protestantism in search of sovereignty. The Parliament of England declared a break-up with Rome, the 1533 Act of Restraint Appeals, and a declaration of England as an independent country, ruled by one head and a king, and all were the consequences of Protestant Reformation. The Protestant Reformation resulted in the emergence of state as a power.

Germany, however, was not able to respond positively to Protestant Reformation. When Luther translated the Bible into the German language, the entire country divided into two parts. As different parts of the country speak different forms of German language, one part was in favor of Protestant Reformation, another in favor of the Catholic. Protestants were quite successful in Scotland, Holland and especially in England.

Protestant Reformation was not in coordination with modern commerce, and industrial development.

CATHOLIC REFORMATION

Catholic Reformation was introduced in 1490, and was based upon the principles of Christian humanity. It is considered to be the rediscovery of the living tradition. Catholic reform was a reply to the Protestants. These reforms were independent of the dissolute renaissance papacy. The earlier phase of the Catholic Reform was unable to face the strong wind of the Protestant Reformation, thus a second phase was started under the leadership of an aggressive papal network and persisted in the middle and other half of the sixteenth century.

RESULT OF CATHOLIC REFORMATION

The Catholic reformers were able to spread literacy and education with the effort of Jesuits. It emphasized the importance of charity. Catholic Europe saw the practice of giving alms, opening orphanages and homes for the poor and needy. Catholic reformation also brought change in the role of women in society. Catholic reformers not only emphasized the education of women, but also preached faith and sacrifice. While the Protestants believed in blind faith and authority of scriptures, Catholic reformers were in favor of the dignity of human existence.

Early Modern Europe, 1560-1648

THE OPENING OF THE ATLANTIC

The Renaissance school explains that the Portuguese and Spanish voyages started during the expansion of Renaissance civilization, and it was only the result of curiosity and independence. Another school explains that the motive behind these voyages was to conquer different parts of Asia and acquire spices and other valuable goods.

During the second half of the fourteenth century, the Portuguese succeeded in establishing colonies in different parts of the Atlantic islands of Azores and Madeira. In the early years of the fifteenth century, they decided to conquer West Africa, as these areas were rich in gold and slaves, and succeeded in discovering different islands, rich in valuables.

The Portuguese started their voyage from Ceuta, in North Africa, and moved towards the coastal area of western Africa. At the end of 1460, the Portuguese managed to control the coastal areas, rich in gold and slaves. Later Bartholomew Dias discovered Cape of Storms, which was later called the Cape of Good Hope by King John II.

In 1497, King Manuel I ordered Vasco da Gama and his fleet to move towards India. The captain with his fleet reached the east coast of Africa, and then after crossing Indian Ocean reached the western region of India. The fleet loaded up a variety of spices and sailed back to their nation. However, quite a few of them were left behind, along with the captain and the spices. The Portuguese found the spices so good that from 1500 onwards, they continued coming to the place for that purpose.

Influenced by the successful Portuguese voyages, Spain also planned to sail and explore different areas and discover different worlds. There are many who doubt that Columbus discovered America.

Historians believe that it was the Vikings who first reached the Western Hemisphere in 1000. Second reason for saying Columbus did not discover America: Columbus before his death was not able to realize that it was a new world, and he thought that the area explored by him was the extended portion of Asia. However, when Columbus returned from his voyage, he had brought gold with him. This further forced the countries to revisit the area to acquire gold and other valuable items.

The discovery of America was not a great thing for Spain as the Portuguese still stood stronger by capturing most of the areas rich in spices. Fighting continued between the two powers, and as a consequence, both managed to capture different parts of the continent.

THE COMMERCIAL REVOLUTION

Capitalism and mercantilism together resulted in commercial revolution. Capitalism is defined as the system in which the production, distribution and exchange are in control of some private hands, so that they can earn maximum profit. Mercantilism emphasized government control over the production, distribution and exchange so that profit can be well spent upon the progress of the state as whole.

There are various elements that factor into the definition of commercial revolution.

Heavy Investment of Capitals
The enterprises realized that growth in business can only be possible through heavy capital investment, which could only be done by increasing the price of agricultural products. But the problem was that the increased price would result in fewer people being able to afford the products, resulting in hunger and thus poor economic growth. However, agricultural businessmen invested huge capital. These investments were later used by the banks for expanding business. This in turn benefited everyone, merchants as well as the investors.

Growth of Banking
Banking had an indecisive reputation in the medieval age, but had great recognition in early modern Europe. The growth of banking led to the development of various financial bodies providing aids to the merchants and entrepreneurs.

Extension of Credit Facilities
With the extension of credit facilities, merchants in any part of Europe could buy goods from merchants based in other parts of Europe by means of a bill issued by an Amsterdam bank. Later, the merchant on the other side would deposit this bill in the local bank and claim money. With the passage of time, cheques were also accepted in the local transaction.

Development of Business Organizations

Another quite important element of capital revolution is the development of business organizations or the regulated companies. This later introduced the concept of Joint Stock Company. The idea of joint stock companies became much more fruitful as it was stable in nature. A large amount of money was collected through shares, which later was invested in the enterprises.

Money Economy

Commercial revolution led to the growth of a money economy.

Disadvantages of Capital Revolution

No doubt, the capital revolution completely revolutionized the concept of business, but it had some disadvantages. Firstly, with the expansion of the enterprises across the globe, there was a hike in the price of silver, which badly effected Europe in the latter half of the sixteenth century. It also led to economic instability. Among the different European countries, the worst sufferers were Spain and Italy.

DYNASTIC AND RELIGIOUS CONFLICTS

In the early years of the sixteenth century, the politics of Europe saw the emergence of nation states and the development of a state system. Moors were thrown out of Spain; in France, kings managed to keep things under their control, and Tudors in England successfully began a dynasty.

Politics in Europe in the early years of the sixteenth century were based upon the dynastic conflicts. Among several European dynasties, the Hapsburg family and their successors managed to stretch their dynasty in Germany, and were recognized as the Holy Roman Empire. Hapsburg's strongest rivals were the Valois kings of France. Though the dynasties of the Valois kings were as wide as those of the Hapsburg's, both had a conflict in the name of Italy.

Both of these dynasties wanted to bring Italy under their control, which resulted in a series of wars and conflicts, and became the basis for the politics of that period. In all the dynastic conflicts, English rulers supported one of the dynasties, and thus weakened the strength of other dynasties.

Religious Conflicts

Religious conflicts made European politics more complicated and disturbing. Since 1517, the unity of the Church in Western Europe was destroyed, and western civilization was badly damaged.

Martin Luther played a great role in bringing an end to some of the old practices, which according to him were against salvation and sacrifices. According to him, salvation can never be achieved through works, but it is only possible by the grace of God. However, his thoughts angered the Church administration, who believed that salvation can only be achieved by performing certain works, and only the Church can decide what those steps are. Thus, they all turned against Luther.

Luther got a huge response from different parts of Europe. Most of the upper middle class people living in the urban areas were tired of the practices of Church, and joined Luther's group. They all were called Protestants.

All these religious conflicts had a great impact on politics as well. Charles V, another Emperor of the Holy Roman Empire, was in favor of the Church and on the other side Henry VIII of England was willing to break his marriage and thus England emerged as a Protestant nation.

In other parts of Europe like Spain and Italy, investigations were carried out to implement support to the Church. However, France had another situation to deal with; the French king, on the basis of an agreement, had complete control over the Church in France. The situation was somewhat different in France. The French king had signed a Concordat with the Papacy that gave him complete control of the French church. Thus rulers had no reason to quarrel with the authority of the Church.

THOUGHT AND CULTURE

The early modern Europe saw great changes in the economic field; however, the society during that time was based upon the old pattern. Citizens were divided into three categories - nobles, clergy and peoples. The members of higher orders were sophisticated and had a very distinct life style, they often resembled the nobility. Merchants and manufacturers too lived in different styles so that they appeared distinct from artisans and peasants.

Three to four percent of Europeans were aristocrats. They had a very royal and sophisticated life. The aristocrat ladies had a unique dressing style. The lifestyle of the aristocrats was different in different countries. In England and Prussia, aristocrats were confined to their estates only, while in Germany and France, aristocrats lived in royal palaces, leaving all of their responsibilities upon the shoulders of the wardens.

Most of the aristocrats owned large provinces and lands. The aristocrats in France owned two of the four coal mines. However, aristocracy never was confined to a particular group of people. If a man had a large amount of money or had estates, he was considered an aristocrat. With the passage of time, several new aristocrats came into existence. They had closer conflict with the old group.

PEASANTRY

Throughout Europe, peasants were not in a good position, and were often heavily supervised under landowners. Landowners - for the sake of gaining more and more profit - forced peasants to work hard, and it seemed that serfdom had again emerged from the past. The condition of the peasants in Western Europe was worse than that of the peasants living in Eastern Europe. In general, the lives of the peasants were very poor, and were full of struggle.

GROWTH OF TOWN AND URBANIZATION

Most of the populations in early modern Europe were dwelling in rural villages. With the passage of time, towns and cities became an indispensable part of this period. The growth rate of urbanization was different in different parts of Europe. The populations of different towns and cities were different on the basis of the availability of capital and income.

The lower segment of the urban society was made up of poor people, who either were porters, unskilled or less skilled workers.

EDUCATION

The method of education differed for different orders. Aristocrats were taught by private teachers, though they occasionally visited universities. There were special training classes for people joining government services. Special methods of teaching were also available for the middle class. There was less provision for the education of peasants and others belonging to the lower order. However, overall, there was an increase in the literacy rate during the time of early modern Europe.

CULTURE

The cultural lives of the people during early modern Europe were quite satisfying and saw substantial growth. The people residing in the rural areas of the Roman Catholic countries were confined to attending church for offering prayers and also gathered there for social occasions. Their religious beliefs and practices gave them a chance to gather and share their things with each other.

Pilgrimages, carnivals and annual harvest festivals were organized so that people could come together, leaving behind all their worries and tension, and provide an occasional dance to enjoy. Taverns too were popular places where the people spent relaxing moments playing games, and occasionally gambling, after the day's long work. All these practices helped in keeping men together companionably.

Western Civilization Since 1648

Since 1648, Western civilization has led the world in many respects. Often that leadership came in the form of discovery, whether that was new lands, new scientific advancements, or new ideas. Sometimes that leadership came from political ideologies that clashed, thereby leading to war. The history of the modern West, therefore, is both captivating and tragic.

Autocracies and Constitutionalism, 1648-1715

The growth of nation-states in Western Europe began as feudalism declined. England and France had developed into highly centralized nation-states by 1500. Spain, only recently unified politically, rapidly and aggressively consolidated royal power, using the influence of the Catholic Church. Their governments were under the leadership of strong rulers, who often reigned as absolute monarchs, that is, the king or queen had complete or absolute rule over the nation and its subjects. Such monarchs are also called autocrats, and their governments are referred to as autocracies.

In Central and Eastern Europe, ethnic and cultural diversity impeded the development of nation-states based on commonalities of language and tradition. The shifting boundaries of the Holy Roman Empire and the widespread holdings of the Habsburg dynasty created more loosely knit political units' resistant to centralization. In addition, the power of the land owning nobility in these areas had been reasserted at the expense of both monarchs and the urban middle class. Unlike the west where the peasantry had maintained the social and economic gains of the late Middle Ages, eastern peasants succumbed to the concerted efforts of landowners to reestablish serfdom.

THE DUTCH REPUBLIC

The first European society to throw off the yoke of a powerful central state, and then to adopt a constitutional republic, was the Netherlands. After decades of resistance against Spanish domination of the "northern provinces," the United Provinces, or the Dutch Republic, gained recognition of their status from the Spanish crown in 1609. Even so, it was not until the Peace of Westphalia (1648), which ended the Thirty Years War, that Dutch independence was confirmed. Dutch political and economic success was grounded in hardheaded practicality and a fierce sense of independence. The government of the United Provinces was unique in Europe, a republic dominated by prosperous middle class merchants who valued thrift, diligence, and simplicity. It was unique, too, because toleration became a cornerstone of Dutch political and economic practice. In a practical sense, toleration attracted investors of all faiths and backgrounds, and the Netherlands profited greatly from this. They also benefited greatly from dominating trade from a neutral status when other European powers were expending finances and resources for warfare on the continent and in overseas colonies. During the remainder of the seventeenth century, the Dutch example would serve as a model for scores of constitutionally-minded people of northern and western Europeans.

FRANCE

While the Dutch were moving away from central power, the French experienced a massive expansion of the state's authority. After the Hundred Years War, royal power in France became more centralized. In addition to the rulers of the 1500s who steadily assumed more authority for the crown, as adviser to King Louis XIII, Cardinal Richelieu (1624-1642), Richelieu laid the foundations for a strong French monarchy by weakening the nobles and increasing taxes. Richelieu made the monarchy absolute within France, and his foreign policy made France the strongest power in Europe.

By the mid-1600s King Louis XIV (1643–1715), who was known as the Sun King, ruled as an absolute monarch. Louis XIV believed in the divine right theory of government, which held that a monarch's power came from God and that the monarch was accountable not to the people he ruled but only to God. Louis also used his wealth for his own benefit rather than for the people. The great palace at Versailles, near Paris, was built at his direction. The construction of the palace seemed to support his statement: "L'état, c'est moi" (I am the state). Not surprisingly, Louis XIV never summoned the Estates-General (the French congress) to meet.

Louis' absolutism also involved waging wars. He led France into many wars, hoping to gain territory. Few of these were successful, and their major result was to increase the dissatisfaction of the French people because of many deaths and high taxes. His control over the French economy was aided by the actions of his finance minister, Jean Colbert.

Louis did promote artistic and musical works to glorify his rule, and in doing so he made France the cultural center of Europe. These activities also increased the spirit of French nationalism. Finally, he revoked the Edict of Nantes, which was a blow to religious freedom and forced many Huguenots to leave France. The absolutism in England and France eventually sparked strong political reactions and resulted in important democratic developments.

ENGLAND

Following the reign of Queen Elizabeth I were the rulers of the Stuart Dynasty (1603–1649), James I and Charles I. They ruled as absolute monarchs, believing they should have no limits set on their power. The Stuart rulers did not respect previous democratic traditions and preferred to rule by divine right. They came into conflict with Parliament because they disregarded it in raising money, imprisoned people unfairly, and persecuted Puritans. However, the underlying conflict was the question of where power would be centered - in the monarchy or in the Parliament.

In 1640, when Scotland invaded England, Charles was forced to call Parliament into session. Led by Puritans, this Parliament, which sat from 1640 to 1660, is known as the Long Parliament, and it changed English history by limiting the absolute powers of the monarchy. In 1641 Parliament denied Charles's request for money to raise an army to fight the Irish rebellion. In response, Charles led troops into the House of Commons to arrest some of its Puritan members. The attempt by Charles to arrest members of Parliament sparked the beginning of the English Civil War (1642-45), as Parliament soon raised an army to fight the king. The Parliamentary forces emerged victorious under the leadership of Oliver Cromwell, a Puritan.

The subsequent Puritan Revolution (1642–1660) included the rule by Oliver Cromwell, which began in 1649. Under Cromwell's leadership, the Parliament voted to abolish the monarchy, and Charles I was tried and beheaded in 1649. England was now a republic or, as it called itself, a commonwealth. However, in 1653, supported by his army, Cromwell took the title of Lord Protector and ruled as a military dictator. His dictatorial policies, which included religious intolerance, strict moral codes, and violence against the Irish, caused resentment. Soon after his death, Parliament invited Charles II, the son of Charles I who was in exile, to take the throne.

Aware of English democratic traditions and the fate of his father, Charles II was careful not to anger Parliament. He acknowledged the rights of the people established by the Magna Carta and the Petition of Right. In 1679, he agreed to the Habeas Corpus Act. On his death in 1685, his brother James II became king. James angered Parliament because of his pro-Catholic actions and his claim to divine right rule. Parliament invited James's older daughter, Mary, and her husband, William of Orange, a Dutch prince who was Protestant, to take the throne.

William and Mary accepted Parliament's offer and arrived in England with an army. They were proclaimed King and Queen, as James II fled to France. As a result of this bloodless revolution, which is known as the Glorious Revolution, Parliament gained in power and prestige. To protect its newly won supremacy over the monarchy, Parliament passed a Bill of Rights that was signed by William and Mary in 1689. By the end of the 17th century, England had become a limited, or constitutional, monarchy, the first in Europe. All the major decisions were made by Parliament, and the ruler's actions were limited by Parliament.

FORMATION OF AUSTRIA AND PRUSSIA

Even though absolutism developed later in Eastern Europe, it proved more enduring, resisting democratic and Enlightenment centered ideas more rigorously right down to the First World War. Weakened by the religious strife in the north during the early 17th century, Austrian rulers of the Holy Roman Empire focused on their lands to the east and south. Ferdinand II (1619–1637) put down a revolt in Bohemia by Czech nobles, redistributed their land, and stamped out Protestantism in the area. Ferdinand III centralized government administration in Austria itself and created a standing army for both defense and domestic control. When the Ottoman siege of Vienna failed in 1683, the Habsburgs, with Russian and other allies, pushed the Turks back and by 1699 controlled Hungary and a large part of Romania.

Complete autocratic centralization was never possible, however, in part because of the vigorous independence of the Hungarian nobility and the lack of a unifying language and culture. Charles VI attempted to guarantee the unity of the three Habsburg realms (Bohemia, Austria, and Hungary) proclaiming in the Pragmatic Sanction (1713) that they should never be divided. The Estates of the three areas, particularly Hungary, continued to strive for influence and resist the power of the crown.

How did a small, landlocked, and relatively unproductive north German kingdom become the core of a militant and powerful empire? The tiny state of Brandenburg, overrun by Swedish and Habsburg armies during the Thirty Years War, and Prussia, tributary state to the King of Poland, were united in 1618 by the Hohenzollern rulers. Formerly a bit player on the stage of the Holy Roman Empire, this dynasty's fortunes changed with the accession to the throne in 1640 of Frederick William, who came to be known as the Great Elector. Taking advantage of an aristocracy weakened by religious wars, and supported by a population tired of the depredations of the marauding armies of Sweden and Poland, he established a standing army and exacted taxes to pay for it. By his death in 1688, Frederick William had consolidated his widely separated lands into a viable, but still small and weak German-speaking kingdom.

It was left to his near-namesake, King Frederick William I (1713–1740) to imbue this new nation-state with an element of his own concept of political power as a function of military might. His strong centralized bureaucracy, coupled with the size and strength of his army precluded significant opposition. He overcame opposition from the great land owning aristocracy of Prussia, the Junkers, by co-opting them into the officer corps, giving them military as well as economic power over other groups in the society. By 1740, Prussia, which ranked twelfth in population, had Europe's fourth largest army - only those of France, Austria, and Russia were larger.

Thus, the "Sparta of the North," as some historians have called it, became a militaristic society where obedience became the primary virtue of the ordinary citizen as well as of the officer or soldier. The precision, skill, and discipline of the Prussian military became the envy of others, and for the next two centuries Prussian arms nearly always prevailed when put to the test of battle.

The "Westernization" of Russia

Under Peter I, usually referred to as "the Great," Russia underwent important changes. Following a policy of Westernization in order to modernize his nation, Peter forced the nobility and upper classes to imitate their counterparts in Western Europe socially and culturally. A Western European-style bourgeoisie (urban middle class) was also created. An enormous civil service and government bureaucracy that drew from both the upper and middle classes was established. Peter encouraged the development of new industries and the importation of Westerners to train Russians. A new capital city, St. Petersburg, was built on the Baltic. Known as the "Window to the West," St. Petersburg was modeled after Western European cities. The Patriarchate was abolished and replaced with the Synod (Council) of Bishops under the control of a Procurator (one of the Tsar's ministers).

The education system, once administered by the Church, was also taken over by the state. The army was modernized, the latest weapons technology imported, and a navy was created. Under Peter, Russia expanded westward to the Baltic and southeast to the Black Sea. For the first time in history, the nation of Russia was no longer landlocked, although both water routes were limited. Even though most of the population were peasants and remained unaffected by the Petrine Reforms, Russia was transformed into a modern world power.

Competition for Empire and Economic Expansion

During the eighteenth century the major European powers - Spain, the Netherlands, France, and England - all worked to expand their territorial holdings in the Americas, Africa, and Asia. That geopolitical contest was deemed crucial because of the economic benefits of producing raw goods from far-flung colonies. As a result, each nation attempted to gain new lands of the others, which in turn produced a series of large-scale wars that not only affected the continent of Europe but also colonies in the Americas and Asia.

Global Economy of the 18th Century

Between the late sixteenth and early nineteenth centuries, the Dutch, French, and English sought to establish colonies in the Americas. They took possession of territory primarily in the Caribbean region and along the northeastern coast of South America. By the eighteenth century, an intricate system of trade among the continents of North America, South America, Africa, and Europe was in place. Generally, Europeans extracted - often through slave labor - raw goods from their colonies in the Americas, and in turn sold finished goods to their colonists across the Atlantic. This system of increasing the size of the economy of the "mother country" by extracting raw goods from colonies was called mercantilism. The establishment of a plantation economy, based on slave labor and restrictive mercantilist trade policies, was promoted by all of the major European powers.

Besides the settlements along the eastern coast of North America, the British were also able to establish themselves throughout the Caribbean. Jamaica, Barbados, and Trinidad-Tobago were their principal possessions in what became the British West Indies in the late 1600s. As had happened elsewhere in the Caribbean, large numbers of African slaves were brought in to provide labor for the sugar-cane plantations in the British West Indies. The first English settlements of South America, in present-day Guyana, began in the 1600s. The English, French, and Dutch colonies in the Caribbean basin all developed a highly profitable sugar-cane-plantation economy, utilizing imported African slave labor. The colonies were controlled by trading policies that favored the "mother" country. The European colonial powers exploited the resources of the Caribbean Islands to further their own economic development. As a result, European nation-states funded their own hyper-expansionist tendencies of the eighteenth century with profits gleaned from their overseas ventures.

Sample Test Questions

An important note about these test questions. Read before you begin. Our sample test questions are NOT designed to test your knowledge to assess if you are ready to take the test. While all questions WILL test your knowledge, many will cover new areas that are not previously covered in this study guide. This is intentional. For questions that you do not answer correctly, take the time to study the question and the answer to prepare yourself for the test.

1) Societies in which people traveled to find food were called what?

   A) Farmers
   B) Indians
   C) Nomads
   D) Cro-magnum
   E) Gypsies

The correct answer is C:) Nomads. Nomads or those in nomadic societies traveled to where they could find food from hunting or gathering natural resources.

2) Much of what scholars know today about early Babylonian civilization is due to which document(s)?

   A) Magna Carta
   B) The Prince
   C) Quaran
   D) Code of Hammurabi
   E) None of the above

The correct answer is D:) Code of Hammurabi. These documents were among the earliest written sets of laws and were assembled the by Babylonian Empire's first ruler, Hammurabi.

3) The first set of laws recorded

   A) Code of Ur-Nammu
   B) Code of Hammurabi
   C) Laws of Eshnunna
   D) Mosaic Laws
   E) Assyrian Laws

The correct answer is B:) Code of Hammurabi. The Code of Hammurabi is said to be the first code of law recorded in 1765 BC. This code is also known as lex talionis, or, "an eye for an eye."

4) Which of the following describes why primogeniture was used in the middle ages?

   A) Because parents naturally favored their oldest son over their other children.
   B) Because parents were only allowed to have one child so no other option was available.
   C) Because the eldest sons threatened their parents and siblings into agreeing with it.
   D) Because inheritance was taxed less if it all passed to one son.
   E) Because land and resources were scarce and needed to be kept together, especially because of the large number of farmers.

The correct answer is E:) Because land and resources were scarce and needed to be kept together, especially because of the large number of farmers.

5) Civilizations can progress when not all members of the society are forced to use all their time to hunt, find or cultivate food. This is called a

   A) Hunting and gathering
   B) Irrigation
   C) Agricultural surplus
   D) Fiefdoms
   E) None of the above

The correct answer is C:) Agricultural surplus.

6) When was Gutenberg's printing press invented?

   A) 1050
   B) 1215
   C) 1440
   D) 1520
   E) 1630

The correct answer is C:) 1440. Gutenberg's printing press revolutionized the information industry. It allowed books to be "mass produced" which allowed the spread of new thought and ideas.

7) Which is the first civilization to have a written language?

   A) Mesoamerican
   B) French
   C) Mesopotamia
   D) Sumeria
   E) Pakistan

The correct answer is D:) Sumeria. Sumeria was the home of the first written language.

8) Who is famed for saying "the ends justify the means?"

   A) Erasmus
   B) Machiavelli
   C) Cosimo Medici
   D) Louis XIV
   E) None of the above

The correct answer is B:) Machiavelli.

9) Which of the following means "to worship multiple gods"?

   A) Monotheistic
   B) Polytheistic
   C) Surplus
   D) Agriculture
   E) None of the above

The correct answer is B:) Polytheistic. The Egyptians were polytheistic.

10) Which was the first civilization to construct arches?

   A) Etruscans
   B) Greeks
   C) Romans
   D) Europeans
   E) None of the above

The correct answer is A:) Etruscans. Although the Etruscans were the first to build them, it was the Romans who adopted them and used them extensively in buildings, bridges and aqueducts.

11) Which of the following civilizations developed the alphabet?

   A) Egyptians
   B) Jews
   C) Phoenicians
   D) Greeks
   E) Sumerians

The correct answer is C:) Phoenicians. The Phoenicians developed the first alphabet by making patterns and sounds. They used this alphabet to communicate with others so they could trade goods.

12) The Thirty Years War occurred in which century?

   A) 13th
   B) 14th
   C) 15th
   D) 16th
   E) 17th

The correct answer is E:) 17th century. The war lasted from 1618-1648.

13) Moses was from which civilization/people?

   A) Egyptians
   B) Jews
   C) Phoenicians
   D) Greeks
   E) Sumerians

The correct answer is B:) Jews. Moses was a great prophet and leader of the Jews.

14) During which of the Punic Wars did Rome gain control of Sicily?

   A) First
   B) Second
   C) Third
   D) Fourth
   E) None of the above

The correct answer is A:) First. The First Punic War began as Rome feared the growing control of the Carthaginian Empire and seized Sicily. There was no Fourth Punic War.

15) Which civilization was the first to develop an agricultural surplus?

   A) Egyptians
   B) Jews
   C) Phoenicians
   D) Greeks
   E) Sumerians

The correct answer is A:) Egyptians. The Egyptians were able to obtain an agricultural surplus because of the very fertile Nile river.

16) Which of the Punic Wars was primarily a naval battle?

   A) First
   B) Second
   C) Third
   D) All of the above
   E) None of the above

The correct answer is A:) First. In the First Punic War Rome fought the Carthaginians for control of the island of Sicily, and control of the surrounding waters.

17) Which writer wrote "The Iliad"?

   A) Tolstoy
   B) Smiths
   C) Troy
   D) Homer
   E) None of the above

The correct answer is D:) Homer. Homer wrote "The Iliad" in approximately 800 BC.

18) Ivan IV of Russia was also known as Ivan the

   A) Great
   B) Powerful
   C) Terrible
   D) Tyrannous
   E) None of the above

The correct answer is C:) Terrible. Ivan the Terrible was the first ruler to be crowned Tsar.

19) Early cities of Mesopotamia were called

   A) Monarchies
   B) Sumer
   C) Greek
   D) Roman
   E) None of the above

The correct answer is B:) Sumer. The early cities of Mesopotamia were called Sumer where they developed into self-governed city states.

20) Which of the following declared Martin Luther a heretic?

   A) Edict of Nantes
   B) Nicene Creed
   C) Council of Trent
   D) Edict of Worms
   E) Magna Carta

The correct answer is D:) Edict of Worms. The Edict was issued after the Diet of Worms in which Luther refused to retract his teachings.

21) Mesopotamia's number one resource was

   A) Gold
   B) Bronze
   C) Water
   D) Silver
   E) Clay

The correct answer is C:) Water.

22) A collection of Marcus Aurelius's thoughts relating to Stoicism was published and called

   A) Ninety Five Theses
   B) Code of Hammaurabi
   C) Meditations
   D) The Prince
   E) None of the above

The correct answer is C:) Meditations. This is a primary source of information about Stoic philosophy.

23) The following picture shows the:

   A) Parthenon
   B) Pantheon
   C) Ziggurat
   D) Sphinx
   E) Pyramid

The correct answer is C:) Ziggurat.

24) Who was the first Russian ruler to be crowned Tsar?

   A) Peter I
   B) Nicholas II
   C) Alexander I
   D) Ivan IV
   E) Catherine II

The correct answer is D:) Ivan IV. Ivan IV was also known as Ivan the Terrible.

25) Which civilization used columns in their architecture of temples?

   A) Greek
   B) Italian
   C) German
   D) Spanish
   E) England

The correct answer is A:) Greek. The Greeks used columns in much of their architecture.

26) Who wrote *The Prince*?

   A) Hammaurabi
   B) Machiavelli
   C) Cosimo de Medici
   D) Joan of Arc
   E) None of the above

The correct answer is B:) Machiavelli. The book was written as Machiavelli's views on what made a good ruler. Many thought it to have been a tribute to his friend, Cosimo de Medici.

27) King Nebuchadnezzar II is most famous for

   A) Great Wall
   B) Coliseum
   C) Sphinx
   D) Pyramids
   E) The Hanging Gardens

The correct answer is E:) The Hanging Gardens. The Hanging Gardens are said to be one of the seven wonders of the ancient world.

28) Which of the following was NOT done at the Council of Trent?

   A) Reaffirmed the doctrine of transubstantiation.
   B) Defended the practice of venerating saints.
   C) Repealed the practice of granting indulgences.
   D) Review and clarify various areas of church doctrine.
   E) All of the above were done at the Council of Trent.

The correct answer is C:) Repealed the practice of granting indulgences. The practice of indulgences was upheld by the Council of Trent.

29) To maintain control of emotions and accept life passively is called

   A) Epicureanism
   B) Cynicism
   C) Marxism
   D) Stoicism
   E) Hedonism

The correct answer is D:) Stoicism.

30) In attempting to strengthen the King's power, which group did Cardinal Richlieu most fight against?

   A) English
   B) Polish
   C) Calvinists
   D) Huguenots
   E) Italians

The correct answer is D:) Huguenots. Although France was primarily Catholic, the Protestant Huguenots controlled a significant amount of political power.

31) Which school of thought advocated seeking as much pleasure as possible

   A) Epicureanism
   B) Cynicism
   C) Marxism
   D) Stoicism
   E) Hedonism

The correct answer is E:) Hedonism. Those who believe in Hedonism believe that pleasure is the most important thing in life.

32) Where did Stoic philosophy originate?

   A) Rome
   B) Italy
   C) Egypt
   D) China
   E) Greece

The correct answer is E:) Greece. Stoicism originated in Greece but was also popular in Rome. The philosophy flourished from 300 BC-300 AD.

33) To seek after the good things in life, but in moderation

   A) Epicureanism
   B) Cynicism
   C) Marxism
   D) Stoicism
   E) Hedonism

The correct answer is A:) Epicureanism.

34) What was the name of the treaty ending the Thirty Years War?

    A) The Peace of Westphalia
    B) The Versailles Treaty
    C) The Second Treaty of London
    D) Treaty of Windsor
    E) Peace of Constance

The correct answer is A:) Peace of Westphalia.

35) This Greek philosophy originally advocated the pursuit of a simple lifestyle

    A) Epicureanism
    B) Cynicism
    C) Marxism
    D) Stoicism
    E) Hedonism

The correct answer is B:) Cynicism. The definition of cynicism has evolved with time, changing from a Greek philosophy to a word that describes a negative or jaded outlook on life.

36) When was the Hundred Years War?

    A) 1337-1453
    B) 1320-1420
    C) 1416-1516
    D) 1298-1398
    E) 1340-1440

The correct answer is A:) 1337-1453. The Hundred Years War technically spanned 116 years, though there wasn't constant fighting.

37) The ruling class of the Romans were known as

    A) Etruscans
    B) Plebeians
    C) Gauls
    D) Patricians
    E) None of the above

The correct answer is D:) Patricians. The Patricians were the ruling class (families) of the Romans. The Plebeians were the common people.

38) During which of the Punic Wars were the Carthaginian people completely destroyed?

   A) First
   B) Second
   C) Third
   D) Fourth
   E) None of the above

The correct answer is C:) Third. The Third Punic War was the final conflict between the Romans and Carthaginians. There was no Fourth Punic War.

39) The Etruscans treated women

   A) Like dogs
   B) As servants
   C) As equals
   D) As goddesses
   E) None of the above

The correct answer is C:) As equals.

40) For which period was the shape of the cross a characteristic shape for churches and monasteries?

   A) Classical
   B) Romanesque
   C) Renaissance
   D) Baroque
   E) Gothic

The correct answer is B:) Romanesque. The period lasted from approximately the 6th to 13th century.

41) When Rome conquered Greece, the Romans Greek culture was:

   A) Destroyed
   B) Adopted
   C) Mocked
   D) Changed
   E) None of the above

The correct answer is B:) Adopted.

42) Which of the following statements is NOT true?

   A) One of Luther's main reasons for writing his Ninety-Five Theses was that he disagreed with the selling of indulgences.
   B) Luther wrote his Ninety-Five Theses to explain why he was breaking away from the Catholic Church.
   C) The Ninety-Five Theses were primarily written to challenge to authority of the Pope.
   D) Both B and C are false
   E) All of the statements are true

The correct answer is D:) Both B and C are false. In fact, when Luther wrote the theses he had no intention of breaking away from the Catholic Church, and he wrote them out of theological concerns. He didn't mean for them to be a challenge to the Pope's authority.

43) Romans small farmers were most likely to produce

   A) Grain
   B) Wine
   C) Olive oil
   D) Textiles
   E) None of the above

The correct answer is A:) Grain. Small farmers were more likely to product grain while the large scale farmers produced olive oil and wine.

44) In which of the following battles were the Greeks victorious?

   A) Battle of Thermoplyae
   B) First Punic War
   C) Battle of Westphalia
   D) Second Punic War
   E) Battle of Marathon

The correct answer is E:) Battle of Marathon. At the Battle of Marathon, the people of Athens successfully delayed the Persian advance into Greece.

45) The river runs through Rome.

    A) Po
    B) Tiber
    C) Nile
    D) Ennis
    E) None of the above

The correct answer is B:) Tiber. The Tiber river runs through Rome.

46) Which religion believed in the doctrine of "sola fide"?

    A) Calvinist
    B) Huguenots
    C) Lutherans
    D) Catholics
    E) None of the above

The correct answer is C:) Lutherans. Lutherans believed that it was faith, not acts or predestination, which determined a person's salvation. "Sola fide" means "only by faith."

47) Cicero was a Roman

    A) Emperor
    B) Artist
    C) Philanthropist
    D) Orator
    E) None of the above

The correct answer is D:) Orator. Cicero was a politician and orator who believed in giving power back to the Republic.

48) Hammurabi ruled which of the following empires?

    A) Babylonian Empire
    B) Mongol Empire
    C) Roman Empire
    D) Ottoman Empire
    E) Macedonian Empire

The correct answer is A:) Babylonian Empire. Hammurabi expanded his kingdom from a few cities to create the Babylonian Empire in 1500 B.C.

49) When was Rome founded?

   A) May 21, 821 BC
   B) April 21, 921 BC
   C) April 21, 753 BC
   D) May 21, 753 BC
   E) None of the above

The correct answer is C:) April 21, 753 BC.

50) Which crop would you NOT find in Europe in the Middle Ages?

   A) Barley
   B) Wheat
   C) Oats
   D) Potatoes
   E) Turnips

The correct answer is D:) Potatoes. Potatoes weren't introduced in Europe until after the discovery of the Americas. Corn would also not be found.

51) According to legend, Rome was founded by

   A) Dionysius
   B) Remus
   C) Spock
   D) Romulus
   E) Regia

The correct answer is D:) Romulus. According to legend, Remus and Romulus were twin brothers who were almost drowned as babies but were rescued and raised by a she-wolf. Romulus later kills Remus, leaving him to found the city.

52) Which of the following best explains the purpose of *The Prince*?

   A) It was Machiavelli's tribute to his father.
   B) It described Machiavelli's political theories on how a ruler maintained power.
   C) It was a book written by Machiavelli describing the past rulers of Italy.
   D) It was Machiavelli's tribute to his good friend and ruler of Florence, Cosimo Medici.
   E) None of the above

The correct answer is B:) It described Machiavelli's political theories on how a ruler maintained power. In it, Machiavelli set forth principles such as "the ends justify the means" and that it is better for a ruler to be feared than loved.

53) Julius Caesar's death resulted in

   A) Celebration
   B) Civil war
   C) Political stagnation
   D) Monarchy
   E) None of the above

The correct answer is B:) Civil war.

54) Which of the following is a true statement about Joan of Arc?

   A) She was a noble born girl who the king chose to lead the French army.
   B) She was a peasant girl who believed she received a call from God to lead the French army.
   C) She was executed by the French clergy on counts of heresy.
   D) She led the French to victory in the Siege of Orleans, but died at the end of the battle.
   E) None of the above

The correct answer is B:) She was a peasant girl who believed she received a call from God to lead the French army. She led the French to victory in the Siege of Orleans but was later captured and executed by the English.

55) About when did the unification of Egypt take place?

   A) 300 BC
   B) 100 BC
   C) 3100 BC
   D) 300 AD
   E) 100 AD

The correct answer is C:) 3100 BC.

56) The Nicene Creed was issued to summarized the primary beliefs of the Roman Catholic Church and specifically address the fact that

   A) Christ would come again.
   B) Belief in church doctrine was essential.
   C) The use of religious images was acceptable.
   D) Christ and God were of one essence.
   E) None of the above

The correct answer is D:) Christ and God were of one essence. Dissentions had arisen from one of the priests, Arius, who believed that there were separate beings.

57) Who built the first pyramids?

   A) Zozer
   B) Gozer
   C) Ahomse
   D) Narmer
   E) None of the above

The correct answer is A:) Zozer. Zoser, the mighty king of United Egypt who ruled around 2770 BC, was regarded as the founder of Old Kingdom and built the first pyramids.

58) In which of the following wars did Rome gain control of Spain?

   A) First Punic War
   B) Second Punic War
   C) Third Punic War
   D) Great War
   E) None of the above

The correct answer is B:) Second Punic War. When the Carthaginians began an offensive against Rome, the Romans went to Spain to cut off their supply. Forced to surrender the Carthaginians had to give up Spain and pay a large sum of money.

59) Which of the following is NOT part of Hammurabi Laws?

   A) Inequality before the law
   B) No distinction between intentional and accidental crime
   C) A person could be sentenced for any crime if not brought to justice by the victim's family
   D) An arm for an arm
   E) None of the above

The correct answer is E:) None of the above. All of the answer choices A-D were a part of the Hammurabi Laws.

60) During which dynasty did Amenhotep I rule Egypt?

   A) 16th
   B) 17th
   C) 18th
   D) 19th
   E) 20th

The correct answer is C:) 18th. He was the second ruler of the 18th dynasty.

61) During the Greek Dark Ages, the barter system

   A) Stayed the same
   B) Was wiped out
   C) Increased in strength
   D) Was replaced by coinage
   E) None of the above

The correct answer is C:) Increased in strength. During the Dark Ages, social and economics were reduced to primitive forms. Barter gained strength as a way of doing business.

62) Who is considered the Father of the Protestant Reformation?

   A) Martin Luther
   B) Huldrych Zwingli
   C) John Knox
   D) John Calvin
   E) None of the above

The correct answer is A:) Martin Luther. Although each was a leader in his own area or belief, Martin Luther was the first to really break away from the church.

63) Athens was primarily of the following EXCEPT

   A) An exporter of agriculture
   B) A business center
   C) A harbor
   D) Rich in mineral deposits
   E) All of the above

The correct answer is A:) An exporter of agriculture. Athens was NOT an exporter of agriculture but was a great business center, contributed to by excellent harbors and mineral deposits.

64) Which position did Cardinal Richelieu serve in?

   A) King
   B) Priest
   C) General
   D) Prime Minister
   E) None of the above

The correct answer is D:) Prime Minister. Cardinal Richelieu served as Prime minister under King Louis XIII, and worked to strengthen his power.

65) Which of the following is NOT a work by Plato?

   A) *The Apology*
   B) *The Phaedo*
   C) *The Phaedrus*
   D) *The Symposium*
   E) None of the above

The correct answer is E:) None of the above. *The Apology*, *The Phaedo*, *The Phaedrus*, *The Symposium* and *The Republic* were all books written by Plato.

66) According to primogeniture, who inherits wealth and property after the parents die?

   A) All of the children split their parent's wealth.
   B) All of the male children split their parent's wealth.
   C) The eldest child inherits everything.
   D) The eldest son inherits everything.
   E) The wealth passes to the government.

The correct answer is D:) The eldest son inherits everything. Primogeniture was normal in the middle ages and under the feudal system.

67) The Edict of Milan gave what granted what in the Roman Empire?

   A) Equality to women
   B) Freedom of religion
   C) The right to appeal
   D) Equal representation
   E) None of the above

The correct answer is B:) Freedom of religion.

68) What is Leonardo da Vinci MOST famous for?

   A) Mona Lisa
   B) The Last Supper
   C) The Baptism of Christ
   D) The Virgin and Child with Saint Anne
   E) Madonna of the Rocks

The correct answer is A:) Mona Lisa. Although all of the works are associated with Leonardo da Vinci, he is most famous for painting the Mona Lisa.

69) The Pope is considered the leader of which religious people?

   A) Christians
   B) Jews
   C) Followers of Islam
   D) Catholics
   E) None of the above

The correct answer is D:) Catholics.

70) Which of the following best describes the background to the Hundred Years War?

   A) A new and ambitious English king had just ascended the throne and received word from a spy network that France planned to invade. He decided to take the first action and start the war.
   B) France became largely divided after the king died and his two sons were fighting for his throne. England decided to take opportunity of France's weak moment.
   C) The English Royalty were descendants of people who had ruled an area of France that had been taken over and wanted to avenge their ancestors.
   D) The French king died with no heir and the English king felt he had a legitimate claim to the throne. A large portion of the French people did not support this claim.
   E) None of the above

The correct answer is D:) The French King died with no heir and the English King felt he had a legitimate claim to the throne. A large portion of the French people did not support this claim.

71) When a person renounces a "worldly life" and dedicates their life to God, this is

   A) Epicureanism
   B) Cynicism
   C) Monasticism
   D) Monarchy
   E) None of the above

The correct answer is C:) Monasticism.

72) During which time period did the Hyksos invade and rule Egypt?

   A) Old Kingdom
   B) Middle Kingdom
   C) Early Kingdom
   D) New Kingdom
   E) Old Kingdom

The correct answer is B:) The Middle Kingdom. The Hyksos ruled from around 1500-1600 BC.

73) Who was also known as "Charles the Great"?

   A) Sophocles
   B) Pope Boniface
   C) Charlemagne
   D) King Charles VI
   E) None of the above

The correct answer is C:) Charlemagne.

74) Which of the following best describes the result of the Battle of Thermoplyae?

   A) The Greeks beat out the Persians and delayed their advance to Athens.
   B) The Persians defeated the Greeks and effectively took control of the area.
   C) Although the Persians technically lost, the battle was only a minor element of their plan to invade and take control of Greece and didn't greatly affect them.
   D) Although the Greeks technically lost, the battle became a symbol of heroism and delayed the Persians to allow continued ship building for a battle on the seas.
   E) None of the above

The correct answer is D:) Although the Greeks technically lost, the battle became a symbol of heroism and delayed the Persians to allow continued ship building for a battle on the seas.

75) Hagia Sophia was a

   A) City
   B) War
   C) Leader
   D) Church
   E) Country

The correct answer is D:) Church. This famous landmark was originally a basilica, then a mosque and now is a museum in Istanbul, Turkey.

76) Which of the following best describes the Magna Carta?

   A) A document which the English King voluntarily signed which instituted a Parliament.
   B) A document which the English King was forced to sign which limited his powers.
   C) A document which the English King wrote which increased the span of his power.
   D) A document which the English King refused to sign because it would limit his power.
   E) A document which the English Parliament passed against the wishes of the King which forced him to obey the laws, and pass all decisions through them.

The correct answer is B:) A document which the English King was forced to sign which limited his powers.

77) The religious text of Islam

    A) Bible
    B) Koran
    C) Tables of Law
    D) Islamic Texts
    E) None of the above

The correct answer is B:) Koran.

78) When was the Council of Trent held?

    A) Just after WWII
    B) Before the Black Plague
    C) As part of the Counter Reformation
    D) After the French Revolution
    E) Just before WWI

The correct answer is C:) As part of the Counter Reformation. The Council of Trent met to discuss, clarify and defend church policy in response of the Reformation.

79) A piece of land used for a vassal's source of income

    A) Lord
    B) Feudal
    C) Fief
    D) Plebian
    E) None of the above

The correct answer is C:) Fief. A lord granted land, or a fief to a vassal who would then work the lord's land and the fief to provide an income for him and his family.

80) The Quaran is the holy book of which religion?

    A) Catholic
    B) Jewish
    C) Muslim
    D) Baptist
    E) Hindu

The correct answer is C:) Muslim. The Quaran is believed to be a series of revelations to the prophet Muhammed.

81) Which of the following is NOT a class of citizen in the medieval society?

    A) Peasant
    B) Merchant
    C) Nobility
    D) Clergy
    E) None of the above

The correct answer is E:) None of the above. All of the above are classes in the medieval society.

82) In which of the Punic Wars were the Carthaginians MOST successful?

    A) First
    B) Second
    C) Third
    D) Fourth
    E) All of the above

The correct answer is B:) Second. In the Second Punic War the Carthaginians were on the offensive, and decimated all of the opposing armies they faced. They lost due to a lack of supplies.

83) Who wrote the *Divine Comedy?*

    A) Dante
    B) Florence
    C) Plato
    D) Sir Thomas Aquinas
    E) St. Francis

The correct answer is A:) Dante. Dante was considered the greatest medieval poet in history. *Divine Comedy* was about a journey through hell.

84) Huguenot was another name for

    A) French Calvinists
    B) English Protestants
    C) French Catholics
    D) English Catholics
    E) English Calvinists

The correct answer is A:) French Calvinists.

85) Who wrote "Summa Theologica"?

    A) Dante
    B) Florence
    C) Plato
    D) Sir Thomas Aquinas
    E) St. Francis

The correct answer is D:) Sir Thomas Aquinas.

86) Which of the following BEST describes the First Council of Nicaea?

    A) A council held in response to the Reformation in which the Nicene Creed was issued.
    B) A council held to advance the Reformation in which the Lutheran church was recognized.
    C) A council of Reformation leaders who met at debated various doctrinal points.
    D) The trial in which Martin Luther was told to renounce his teachings and refused.
    E) None of the above

The correct answer is A:) A council held in response to the Reformation in which the Nicene Creed was issued. The Nicene Creed primarily stated that God and Jesus Christ were of the same essence.

87) Which of the following a significant influence in constitutional government?

    A) Summa Theologica
    B) Divine Comedy
    C) Magna Carta
    D) Koran
    E) Tables of Law

The correct answer is C:) Magna Carta. The Magna Carta was written in England and gave English subjects of the King specific legal rights such as allowing appeals.

88) Which of the following was depicted on the Normandy Bayeux Tapestry?

   A) The Norman Conquest
   B) The Norman rulers from 750-1200 AD
   C) A collection of Norman folk stories
   D) The early constitution of Normandy
   E) None of the above

The correct answer is A:) The Norman Conquest. The Norman Conquest was when William the Conqueror successfully invaded England in the mid-11th century.

89) The Black Plague was spread by

   A) Produce
   B) Fleas and rats
   C) Improper hand washing
   D) Tainted meat
   E) Restrooms

The correct answer is B:) Fleas and rats. The Black or Bubonic Plague was responsible for killing over 30% of the population.

90) Which of the following statements about the Thirty Years War is true?

   A) The Bohemian Phase of the war was the longest and most brutal phase, and was ended by the Peace of Westphalia.
   B) The fighting of the War took place mainly in present day Poland.
   C) It was ended by the Second Treaty of London, signed in 1638.
   D) Although it began as a conflict between Catholics and Protestants, it eventually evolved into a fight for political power among the major ruling families of Europe.
   E) None of the above

The correct answer is D:) Although it began as a conflict between Catholics and Protestants, it eventually evolved into a fight for political power among the major ruling families of Europe. The fighting took place mainly in present day Germany.

91) Agriculture has been a major contribution to civilization and mankind, when was the first recording of agriculture, known as the agricultural revolution?

A) 4000 BC
B) 2700 BC
C) 5000 BC
D) 9500 BC
E) 6000 BC

The correct answer is D:) 9500 BC. 9500 BC, when the Sumerians first began farming.

92) Which of the following statements is TRUE?

A) Calvinists believed that all people would be saved.
B) Lutherans supported the sale of indulgences to finance church projects.
C) Lutherans believed that charitable works were essential to a person's salvation.
D) Calvinists believed that it was through faith that a person could be saved.
E) None of the above

The correct answer is E:) None of the above. Calvinists believed that whether or not a person would be saved was predetermined and couldn't be changed. Lutherans believed that faith was the only important factor in salvation, and disagreed with the sale of indulgences.

93) Who sculpted "David"?

A) Da Vinci
B) Michelangelo
C) Leonardo
D) Sir Thomas Aquinas
E) None of the above

The correct answer is B:) Michelangelo.

94) Which Roman emperor was influenced by Stoicism?

- A) Vespasian
- B) Septimus Severus
- C) Marcus Aurelius
- D) Tiberius
- E) Didius Julianus

The correct answer is C:) Marcus Aurelius. A collection of his thoughts was published as Meditations. It strongly reflects Stoic philosophy.

95) A painting on plaster walls or ceilings

- A) Sistene
- B) Oil based
- C) Pictograph
- D) Fresco
- E) None of the above

The correct answer is D:) Fresco. Frescos were very prevalent during the Renaissance period.

96) The word polis is the Greek equivalent of

- A) Police
- B) Politics
- C) Home
- D) City state
- E) Government

The correct answer is D:) City state. The city states of Greece began to develop around 800 BC.

97) Who believed that salvation came through faith, not works?

- A) John Calvin
- B) Martin Luther
- C) Henry VIII
- D) Sophocles
- E) Sir Thomas Aquinas

The correct answer is B:) Martin Luther. Martin Luther was the founder of Lutherism.

98) For what period were flying buttresses a characteristic architectural feature?

    A) Classical
    B) Romanesque
    C) Renaissance
    D) Baroque
    E) Gothic

The correct answer is E:) Gothic. A buttress is a supporting beam angling outward from a building. Many of the great cathedrals of Europe were designed in the Gothic period.

99) Columbus was financed by the heads of what country?

    A) Italy
    B) Germany
    C) Portugal
    D) Spain
    E) England

The correct answer is D:) Spain.

100) In what year was the Magna Carta issued?

    A) 1052
    B) 1215
    C) 1350
    D) 1512
    E) 1680

The correct answer is B:) 1215. The Magna Carta was the first document forced on the king by his subjects, and forced him to accept certain policies which protected the people's rights.

Test Taking Strategies

Here are some test-taking strategies that are specific to this test and to other CLEP tests in general:

Keep your eyes on the time. Pay attention to how much time you have left.

- Read the entire question and read all the answers. Many questions are not as hard to answer as they may seem. Sometimes, a difficult sounding question really only is asking you how to read an accompanying chart. Chart and graph questions are on most CLEP tests and should be an easy free point.

- If you don't know the answer immediately, the new computer-based testing lets you mark questions and come back to them later if you have time.

- Read the wording carefully. Some words can give you hints to the right answer. There are no exceptions to an answer when there are words in the question such as always, all or none. If one of the answer choices includes most or some of the right answers, but not all, then that is not the correct answer. Here is an example:

  The primary colors include all of the following:

  Red, Yellow, Blue, Green
  Red, Green, Yellow
  Red, Orange, Yellow
  Red, Yellow, Blue
  None of the above

  Although item A includes all the right answers, it also includes an incorrect answer, making it incorrect. If you didn't read it carefully, were in a hurry, or didn't know the material well, you might fall for this.

- Make a guess on a question that you do not know the answer to. There is no penalty for an incorrect answer. Eliminate the answer choices that you know are incorrect. For example, this will let your guess be a 1 in 3 chance instead.

What Your Score Means

Based on your score, you may, or may not, qualify for credit at your specific institution. At University of Phoenix, a score of 50 is passing for full credit. At Utah Valley University, the score is unpublished, the school will accept credit on a case-by-case basis. Another school, Brigham Young University (BYU) does not accept CLEP credit. To find out what score you need for credit, you need to get that information from your school's website or academic advisor.

You can score between 20 and 80 on any CLEP test. Some exams include percentile ranks. Each correct answer is worth one point. You lose no points for unanswered or incorrect questions.

 ## Test Preparation

How much you need to study depends on your knowledge of a subject area. If you are interested in literature, took it in school, or enjoy reading then your studying and preparation for the literature or humanities test will not need to be as intensive as someone who is new to literature.

This book is much different than the regular CLEP study guides. This book actually teaches you the information that you need to know to pass the test. If you are particularly interested in an area, or feel like you want more information, do a quick search online. We've tried not to include too much depth in areas that are not as essential on the test. Everything in this book will be on the test. It is important to understand all major theories and concepts listed in the table of contents. It is also very important to know any bolded words.

Don't worry if you do not understand or know a lot about the area. With minimal study, you can complete and pass the test.

To prepare for the test, make a series of goals. Allot a certain amount of time to review the information you have already studied and to learn additional material. Take notes as you study, it will help you learn the material.

Legal Note

All rights reserved. This Study Guide, Book and Flashcards are protected under US Copyright Law. No part of this book or study guide or flashcards may be reproduced, distributed or stored in a retrieval system, or transmitted in any form or by any means, electronic, mechanical, photocopying, recording, or otherwise, without the prior written permission of the publisher Breely Crush Publishing, LLC. This manual is not supported by or affiliated with the College Board, creators of the CLEP test. CLEP is a registered trademark of the College Entrance Examination Board, which does not endorse this book.

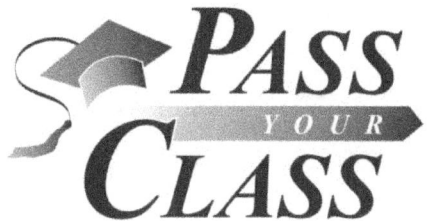

FLASHCARDS

This section contains flashcards for you to use to further your understanding of the material and test yourself on important concepts, names or dates. Read the term or question then flip the page over to check the answer on the back. Keep in mind that this information may not be covered in the text of the study guide. Take your time to study the flashcards, you will need to know and understand these concepts to pass the test.

What was the lifeline of the Egyptian Civilization?	Mesopotamia is Greek for what?
Six Eras of Egyptian History	Zoser
Ramses III	Hammurabi
Law of Retaliation	Was there a distinction between intentional or accidental crime?

Between two rivers	The Nile
Founder of the old kingdom	The archaic or early dynastic period, the Old Kingdom, the 1st Intermediate period, Middle Kingdom, 2nd Intermediate period, the New Kingdom
Gave law to mankind	Last great Pharaoh of Egypt
No	Eye for an eye, etc.

What was the chief source of income for most in the dark ages?	Areopagus
Two achievements of Athens	Atomists
Democritus	Sophits
Pericles	Patricians

Council of Nobles	Agriculture
Philosophers	Vineyards an Olive Yards
A group that opposed slavery and racial discrimination	Denied existence of spiritual world
Upper class landlords, aristocrats, etc.	Formed the first truedemocracy in Athens

Plebians	**Punic Wars**
Julius Caesar	**Who was one of the Five Good Emperors?**
Three civilizations from the Mediterranean Sea?	**Church of Santa Sophia**
Byzantines were famous for?	**Mosaic**

Rome vs. Carthage	Small businessmen, farmers
Marcus Aurelius	Ruled Rome - was assassinated by peers in 44 BC
Byzantine piece of architecture	Byzantine, Islam, Western Christian
A mosaic is a picture made up from small pieces of glass or stone	Ivory paintings, jewelry making and mosaics

Muhammad

Islamic Philosophy

Islamic Inventions

Faylasufs

Charlemagne

Carolingian Renaissance

Beowulf

Book of Kells

Based on Aristotle and Napoleon	Founder of Islam
Islamic Philosophers	Papermaking, distillation of alcohol
A cultural and legal revival led by Charlemagne	Emperor of the Roman, King of the Franks
Irish book of art/calligraphy	Epic poem

Important Farming Tools

Paris became famous for

Venice became famous for

Milan became famous for

Magna Carta

Thomas Becket

Francis Petrarch

Petrarch believed in

| University and education | Heavy plow, horse shoes, horse collars |

| Garment production | Outside trade |

| Archbishop of Canterbury - later became a saint | A series of promises made by King John regarding how to treat his subjects |

| Simple life and meditation | First Renaissance scholar in Italy |

Italian Renaissance Discoveries

Leonardo da Vinci

Michelangelo painted

Michelangelo sculpted

Pieta

Capitalism

Sir Thomas Moore wrote

Pierre Lescot

| A "true" renaissance man | Linear Perspective, human anatomy and oil painting |

| David | Sistine Ceiling |

| An economic system where goods and services are exchanged | A piece of art with Christ upon his mother's lap |

| French architect | Utopia |

Machiavellie	**Mediations**
First Punic War (264-241 BC)	**Ivan the Terrible**
Magna Carta	**Feudal System**
Persio	**Leonardo da Vinci**

A collection of Marcus Aurelius's thoughts which show a view of Stoicism.	A central political theorist of the Renaissance who is famous for writing The Prince.
A cruel ruler of Russia who was the first to be crowned Tsar.	A conflict between Rome and the Carthaginian in which Rome seized Sicily and demonstrated their naval power.
A governing system based on a obligations between kings, lords, knights and peasants.	A document issued in 1215 which attempted to limit the powers of the King of England.
A leading figure of the Renaissance who was an admired painter and is considered a genius. Most known for the Mona Lisa.	A great empire which controlled much of the Middle East and peaked around 500 BC.

First Council of Nicaea

Council of Trent

Huguenot

Chiaroscuro

Joan of Arc

Gothic Architecture

Romaneque Architecture

Stoicism

A meeting held by the Roman Catholic Church in the mid 16th century which affirmed church doctrine	A meeting called by the Roman emperor Constantine in which the Nicene Creed was adopted.
A painting style developed during the Renaissance which uses shading.	A name given to French Calvinists.
A period lasting from the 12th to 16th century in which many of the great cathedrals of Europe were built.	A peasant girl who led the French to victory in the Battle of Orleans. She was later captured and executed by the English.
A philosophical view which emphasized fate and acting with virtue.	A period lasting from the 6th to 13th century which made use of the cross shape for churches and monasteries.

Ninety Five Theses	**Flying buttress**
Hundred Years War	**Code of Hammurabi**
Normandy Bayeux Tapestry	**Battle of Thermopylae**
Battle of Marathon	**Edict of Worms**

A supporting beam angling outward from a building characteristic of the Gothic period.	A statement by Martin Luther about problems he saw within the Catholic Church.
Among the earliest written sets of laws which was assembled by Hammurabi.	A war between France and England in which England attempted to take control of France which lasted 116 years.
Battle in which the Greeks were defeated, but which became a symbol of heroism.	An embroidered tapestry which depicts the story of the conquest of William the Conqueror (the Norman Conquest).
Declared Martin Luther a heretic and placed him outside protection from the law.	Battle in which the people of Athens defeated the advancing Persian army.

Hammurabi	**Third Punic War (149-146 BC)**
Calvinism	**Lutheranism**
John Calvin	**Martin Luther**
Corn	**Potato**

Fearing the Carthaginians would rebuild strength the Romans either enslaved or killed all of them.	Expanded his kingdom from a few cities to create the Babylonian Empire.
Founded by Martin Luther and based on the idea of justification by faith alone	Founded by John Calvin and based on the idea of predestination.
Founder of Lutheranism whose Ninety Five Theses challenged many Catholic teachings.	Founder of Calvinism.
Introduced in Europe after discovery of the Americas.	Introduced in Europe after discovery of the Americas.

Printing Press	**Nicene Creed**
Thirty Years War	**Richelieu**
Marcus Aurelius	**Predestination**
The Prince	**Second Punic War (218-202 BC)**

Issued in response to dissentions, the creed stated that God and Jesus Christ were of the same essence.	Invented in 1440 by Johannes Gutenberg which allowed new ideas to become widespread.
Prime Minister of France under Louis the XIII who worked to strengthen the King's rule.	Lasting from 1618-1648 this war began as a conflictbetween Protestants and Catholics in the HRE.
The belief that who will and will not be saved has already been determined by God, and salvation cannot be earned.	Roman emperor in the second century who was influenced by Stoicism
The Carthaginians had built up their strength in Spain and proceeded to decimate Rome, however when Romans conquered Spain it left the Carthaginian army without support and they were forced to surrender.	The vook was written as Machiavelli's views on what made a good ruler.

Etruscan arches	**Polis**
Quaran	**Primogeniture**
Counter Reformation	**Reformation**
Peace of Westphalia	**Empress Theodora**

The Greek equivalent of "city state" which were the Greek political units centered in single cities.	The Etruscans were the first to build arches but they were adopted and widely used by the Romans.
The practice of having the eldest son inherit everything.	The holy book of the Muslim religion. Also spelled Koran.
The time period in which the power of the Catholic Church declined as new church were formed.	The reaction of the Catholic Church to the Reformation such as the Nicene Council and Diet of Worms.
Wife of Justinian I (Byzantine ruler) who was influential in his policies and effectively saved his empire.	Treaty which ended the Thirty Years War between France and England.

NOTES

NOTES

NOTES

NOTES

NOTES

NOTES

NOTES

NOTES

NOTES

NOTES

NOTES

NOTES

NOTES

NOTES

NOTES

NOTES

NOTES

NOTES

NOTES

NOTES

NOTES

NOTES